Forest Pathways

Ramblings From
The New Forest and Beyond

Michael Forester

First published in Great Britain in 2023
by Paralight Press

www.michaelforester.co.uk

The right of Michael Forester to be identified as author of this work
has been asserted by him in accordance with the Copyright, Designs
and Patents Act 1988

ISBN: 978-1-8380114-2-0

PARALIGHT

PRESS

These words are a river and cannot be turned back.

Andrew Miller
The Slowworm's Song

Reader Feedback for Michael Forester's Forest series

Nothing seems more important than my swift response to receiving Forest Rain through the post. Thank you for writing it. I feel so honoured to have a copy. I am halfway through reading it and I cannot put it down. My soul is responding, knowing that this is one of the great books of all time.

Katherine, UK

I'm reading Forest Rain (couldn't sleep) – undergoing a very emotional healing as I weep for my mother, my family, myself, lost love, missed opportunities.

Caroline, UK.

This is not a book like any other I have read. Mankind has been looking for this message for a very long time. I urge you to clear your mind. Turn your phone off, turn the television off, turn the radio off. Change into your most comfortable clothes, grab a box of tissues, and get comfortable in your favorite reading space. As you read Forest Rain, listen not only to Michael's words, but pay attention to the emotions and self-examination you experience. Soon, you will start to see beyond Michael's experiences, and you will start to see your own.

Ann, California

A wonderful read! There are a lot of life lessons to be learned from the different stories in this book. I would recommend this to anyone who's on a journey of finding their soul!

Rachel, UK

Forest Rain simply touched the recesses of my soul. I could not help but shed tears as I pondered upon each word, each line, each paragraph and the whole of the essays and so with every word, every line, every stanza of each of the poems. I could not even refrain from rereading it the nth time. And each time I do, the effect is be the same.

Janet Pascual, Philippines

Reading Forest Rain allowed me to re-evaluate my current position in life and to seek peace with the flaws that I have yet to forgive myself for. The book is beautifully written, with many insights and valuable lessons that readers can carry with them in their everyday life. For someone who seeks to find clarity, peace and understanding, I would highly recommend Forest Rain, for your heart will be touched and you will learn to flourish in the journey that awaits you. The books serves as a brilliant inspiration for those who seek to mend their souls and find peace with themselves.

Sarah Soon, Philippines

…and the next thing I knew, I was falling at the deepest pit of this book that made it so hard for me to put it down. As I was reading this book, I'm not that aware on how the author himself touches my soul, like what he had mentioned in the first part of this book. I just realised it the moment I felt my own tears drenching my cheeks.

Janel Ranola, Philippines

I would ask yourself the question "Can you love yourself at this time in this life?" This book will give you a deep understanding of yourself and self-realisation of your worth to others.

Susan Aldworth, UK

If you care about the world, you need to read this book. It will open doors in your heart and mind.

Di, UK

I feel like I was meant to read this book. I cannot put it down. I feel like somebody is looking out for me and knew I should find this book. It is the kind of book you need to hold on to as it is relevant in everybody's lives.

Remarla, UK

By reading Forest Rain, I finally answered the question "Who am I?"

Karl, Philippines

Forest Rain is riddled with excellent writing, beautifully communicated, and luxuriously gift-wrapped for our senses. The author is inviting us deeper into his own personal world, opening up doors that few writers would dare to reveal. We start page one as a stranger and become a trusted friend long before the final line is done. This is not a book saying, "Listen to me!"... it's two people chatting about life in front of a pub log fire, safe and secure in the knowledge that we are in the finest company, and all is well with the world ... able to broach any subject.

Kevin Milsom
Reviewing for Inkpantry.com

I could not help but ponder upon every word, paragraph, chapter of the whole book. Through this spiritual book you can discover the astounding, deep and profound messages that signify to you alone.

Emily, Philippines

Forest Rain has washed me deep with its radiance and beauty. It is rejuvenating and life-giving. I read it for the second time and each time the journey inward has been illuminating and profound. Such is the beauty of the writer's expressions that once we immerse into its depth we can't leave it until we experience the entire journey revealed so beautifully.

Sangeeta, Assam, India

Each carefully crafted essay and poem carries a stream of messages via positive metaphors and symbolism. The description of a dream leads to a lesson in forgiveness. A childhood memory of a spider focuses on the myriad of choices we face in this lifetime. The recollection of a faulty wire in a garage door looks into angels and God's sense of humour. Michael's talent as a writer is both simplistic and genius; he draws the reader in like a magnet. We're never pulled in, but merely guided by Michael's total command of the written word.

Kevin Milsom,
Reviewing for Inkpantry.com

CONTENTS

1 When I Am Sleeping

"It's been a long time," she said. Then she paused, waiting for my reply. "I was ready for you," she continued, when I did not answer. "I dressed special for you – put on my finest. You always say autumnal colours suit me best. But you didn't come."

It was an expression more of disappointment than accusation. I shifted my weight from foot to foot, feeling uncomfortable as I looked down at the decaying leaves. "And now look," she said in her sadness, gesturing about herself. "It's almost all gone." I looked up, knowing she was right. There was a quiet, muted sleepiness about her, as if her mind was elsewhere.

"I wanted to come," I began. "I intended to come – really." She waited for more but embarrassment made the words stick in my throat. I was in the wrong, without excuse.

"But you had more important things to do?" she ventured.

I drew my breath in sharply. "No," I replied, not that. Never that. Nothing is more important than coming to be with you."

"Why then?"

I fell silent again. "It's hard to explain," I said, eventually. "There's been a listlessness about me. A drop in my energy. I've not been able to motivate myself. I can't explain why."

"I know what you mean," she said, gesturing to the waning colour of late autumn. The branches of the trees were becoming visible, where just a week or so ago they would have been wrapped in a coat of colour.

"I was depressed," I confessed finally, "I couldn't motivate myself to come to you." I knew how weak it sounded. She waited for more but I had nothing else to add. The silence stood between us like a wall, a barrier forbidding me to step across.

"I'm still here for you," she responded, finally. "I will always be here for you. You do know that, don't you? Just like you know you always feel better when you come to me."

She was right. Whenever I shake off the bonds of lethargy to walk with her, it's like she wakens my soul. I become aware, not just of her and the creatures she tends to, but of the Spirit that moves the heart in her and beyond her. And when I'm lucky enough, or open enough, or maybe just ready enough, that Spirit begins to move me too and, if I'm willing to listen, to open up the truth that dwells behind the illusion.

So, I walked her paths again and the silence that had been a wall became a lovers' bridge as I watched her prepare her children and herself for sleep.

When it was time for me to go, I turned to walk away. Then she spoke again. "Don't leave it so long next time. Come back when I am sleeping, when the snow hangs heavy on my boughs. Come and be with me in the silence. You know that it is in the silence that you find yourself again."

And we both knew she was right.

2 The Right Way to Live

I came to a place where many roads met and sat down on a bench. My angel appeared, as he often does at these times, and we fell into deep conversation, such that I did not notice a stranger approaching.

"Excuse me," said the traveller, drawing near. "Is this the right way to live?"

I looked up, surprised to be addressed during our meditation. It took me a few moments to take in his dishevelled appearance. His clothes were obviously worn out and he was perspiring profusely. It was, after all, a particularly warm day. I smiled at him. "I'm sorry, I didn't catch what you said." I replied.

"I'm wondering if you're going to Live and, if so, can you tell me which of these is the right way?" He gestured to the many roads that met at the point where we were sitting.

"What makes you ask?" I said, a little confused, not sure I was getting his drift.

"Well, I want to get to the town of Live," replied the traveller, "but I think I might have lost my way. You see, I've been told that if I can find the right way to Live all my problems will melt away and I'll be happy. I surmise that the town of Live must be a truly wonderful place and I would really like to get there as soon as possible. So I ask again, can you tell me the right way to Live, please?"

I looked at my angel, then back at the traveller. "I think you might have misunderstood what you have been told," I said. "I know of no town called Live. Living is a process, a journey, a way of being."

"This is the right way to Live," came a voice from behind. I turned to see a middle-aged woman standing behind our bench. "This is the right way to Live," she repeated, pointing unmistakably to one of the roads. I was about to respond, when there came another voice from my left.

"No, ma'am," said a man's voice. "That might be *a* way to Live, but *this* is certainly a much *better* way to Live." I turned to see a tall, earnest-looking young man, pointing determinedly at a different road.

"No, you're both wrong," came a third, emphatic voice from the other side of me. "I've being going to Live for nigh on twenty years now, and I can assure you this is the best way."

"You're all wrong!" came a high-pitched voice from behind me sounding quite irritated. "I have a book here that discloses the only right way to Live. Everyone should be doing what my book instructs." I turned to see a young woman, dressed entirely in black, striding determinedly towards the group, holding a big, black book in her outstretched hand. "In fact," she continued, "I have these short extracts that I have copied out from my book for everyone here. Read my tracts and come with me. Together we'll follow the right way to Live and I'll continue to give you guidance as we proceed. We'll soon reach our destination if you all do exactly as I tell you." She pushed a little pamphlet right under the nose of the traveller who had asked the original question. He shrank back in surprise – well you would, wouldn't you?

"Don't be ridiculous," called another man who was now approaching rapidly. I felt sorry for him, dressed as he was in long, heavy robes with his shaven head exposed to the heat of the sun. "I've read your book from cover to cover and it taught me nothing of value about the right way to Live. But I have great news," he said, fingering the many strings of beads that hung around his neck. "After years of painstaking study and deep thought, I have found a much better way to Live. And today, folks, is your lucky day. I have recorded a series of audio tapes that set out clearly my recommended way to Live and packaged them in an attractive plastic box. I have copies here for you all. Buy my tapes today for just £300 and I'll also give you a copy of my widely acclaimed book at no charge. These tapes and my book will definitely show you a better way to Live than any of you have ever discovered before. But I can't keep this offer open for long, friends. You must buy my tapes today." He took out some brightly coloured plastic boxes from underneath his robes and began proffering them to the group.

"Poppycock!" came a voice from behind him. The woman that owned it was dressed in an expensive-looking business suit with padded shoulders. Her hair was carefully coiffured and her perfume wafted over to us on the breeze. "You're a charlatan. I paid a fortune for your tapes years ago." She put a hand on the speaker's shoulder and pulled him roughly out of her way. "Don't listen to a word he's saying," she said, addressing the rest of the group. "His tapes are useless old technology – a complete waste of money. But don't worry. After continuing my search I have finally found the only way to Live and I have recorded a series of podcasts all about it. A fee of £6,000 split into three easy credit card payments will gain you access to my website where you can watch the podcasts at your preferred time. I know you'll all agree that it's a paltry sum for discovering, finally, what is, in truth, the *only* way to Live."

The voices about us were rising and growing angry as the people argued about the right way to Live. My angel and I got up from the bench and walked a short distance away, to where the poor traveller was standing, looking completely bemused.

My angel looked at me and shook his head. "What a way to live," he said.

3 Bonding in Anderwood

So, we come to Anderwood where the tall Scots pines reach up to eternity. We have come to watch the love of my life as once more she begins to prepare herself for her long sleep. We have eyes only for her as she goes about her bedding ritual. A mattress of coarse bracken she has laid upon the earth and now she begins to quilt it with the first dry leaves that tumble down in the early autumn winds.

The deciduous trees remain green for a little longer yet, reaching out to the last days of the sun, imploring him to stay about a little longer. But he will decline, that sun, for he is a travelling man, a wanderer upon the face of the Earth. He bestows his favours for but a season before moving on to wrap his joy about the shoulders of other lovers. Soon he will flee across the sky and my love will swaddle her silence with the winds while she awaits the coming of the frosts that call her to sleep.

We make our way up towards the Bolderwood Grounds, skirting the edge of the North Oakley Inclosure, crossing Blackensford Brook at the ford where man-made interventions direct the flow of the water. We prefer our flow less overtly controlled, as does the brook down below the ford, where we descend via Smoky Hill to cross back near Woolfield Cottage.

These Forest cottage dwellers are solitary. Their dogs warn of our impending arrival long before we reach their high fences. "Pass on," they bark, "you are not wanted here." So, we walk on until we arrive back at Anderwood where we observe the empty car park and the unattended barbecue tables that you can hire by dialling 0300 067 4601. But that number will not be dialled today. For the tourists have all gone home and we have no desire to char the flesh of the once-living.

Sleep safely, my love. When the snow lies upon your curving uplands, we will walk your leafless lanes and wander only where the woodland creatures sleep within your nurturing arms.

We return to the car and rejoin civilisation at the A35, marvelling that we are just two minutes away from a place where we have walked for two hours and seen no one. Then we proceed to an altogether more populated car park at Lyndhurst, which styles itself 'the capital of the New Forest.' Lyndhurst would seduce us with its Tourist Information Centre and its Forest Museum. We have fallen for their charms many times before but today we are having none of it. We make directly for Costa where the unique blend of Arabica beans temps us to falling once more. We are easily separated from our £3.90 in exchange for a cup of coffee so large it has two handles to hold it, accompanied by two slices of brown buttered toast. We note with fleeting interest our own preference for cremated bread over charred flesh.

We work on 'Bonding'; not the activity, you understand, but the new short story we are writing. When Matt has had enough, he shivers to indicate his distaste for Costa, pathos being his superpower. But he recovers remarkably quickly as soon I make ready to leave. Back in the car park we check out the Community Hall which is advertising its coming Teddy Bear Fair. We decline attendance, leaving others to bond with, and over, teddies. As we turn to leave we are approached by Jan, whose job evidently includes emptying the car park waste bins. We express profound gratitude to Jan and her colleagues, for what would our forest look like without someone to do their job? She falls for Matt instantly, charming him with a solitary dog biscuit. He is as fickle as the waning sun. As they bond over the biscuit I proffer a bookmark promoting our book, *If It Wasn't For That Dog*. Jan is smitten and wants a copy immediately. I return to the car for one. She is delighted when I offer to sign it for her. We wave to her as we drive from the car park, observing that she walks a little taller than when we first saw her. We have evidently been as important in her day as she has in ours. Perhaps in her next lifetime she will be a tall Scots pine, tempting the sun to stay a little longer in Anderwood.

4 Man's Work

Until he extends the circle of all living things, man himself will not find peace.

Albert Schweitzer

Kulturphilosophie,

1923

Her prize discovered in her jaws,
she hangs her head in half feigned guilt
and drops it where she stands.

'This is *Man's Work,*' you say, and walk away.

Conspiratorially, I answer nothing,
but turn for the door
half wishing I were not summoned to do
Man's work.

Head bent half a turn beyond nature's intent,
quivering on the ground, still living beyond probability;
a single eye shines half bright,
pleading with me not to do
Man's Work.

Half a brick thrown down hard from high
half disconnects me from the act,

stuns in one blow, kills in two,
completing all of
Man's work.

A half streak of blood on a half a brick
confirms all life extinguished.
There is no half-life in the afterlife.

If it is woman's work to bear a life and
man's work
to extinguish it,
whose work is it
to weep
for the eyes
that go on shining?

Some suffer too much, others too little.
Buddha

5 Voice of the Turtle

It has been a harsh and silent winter. The energy has slept, voiceless, under the snow blanket for longer than I am used to. It has become difficult to believe that green shoots will ever emerge. The words that cascade through the Summerlands have not come. I have been unable to write for some time now, perhaps for many months – I cannot remember how long. No poetry; no prose. Each attempt produces jagged, awkward phrases, malformed paragraphs and stanzas that hide in shame from the angry eyes of judgement. My blog has languished unposted and my online entries have been confined to old material, eliciting kind comments from those who understand there are times when we cannot be creative.

But winter is a season familiar to me. And I have learned that instead, I must devote my time to the practicalities of being an independent author, selling and distributing my existing work.

Today, we visited the New Forest town of Fordingbridge to drop off stock at a local landmark, Fordingbridge Bookshop. Job complete, we take an hour out to walk at Frogham Common, where we used to walk daily when we lived here, some years ago. Nothing has changed. Matt seems to remember the place. Time was when he would rush about this Common in an interminable frenzy of rabbit chasing, both imaginary and real. I am relieved to say that in his whole life he has never caught anything. It does not matter to him. The joy is in the chase. But now he is old, ninety-nine in dog years, and we no longer live in Frogham. He is content, for the most part, to walk beside me, disappearing momentarily into the gorse, drawn by some lingering shadow-memory of the almost-caught that is the preoccupation of the rapidly ageing, whether we be canine or human.

We turn to head back, but not before we visit the iconic Royal Oak pub at Gorley, where one of us consumes a traditional New Forest Ploughman's lunch. I shall not disclose which of us it was. Then it is time to make our way south again, towards the coast and home, where I shall prepare for next week's visit to the Hay-on-Wye Festival.

Writing is returning to me, now; just a little you understand. It feels like the early spring arriving in the high country. Skeletons begin to solidify when Spirit stirs the dust, as it did to form the first man. Background concepts come into focus. Paragraphs of dialogue begin to crystallise. Renewed creativity, like the first snowmelt, is sweet but it is slow to reach the low country of the pen. Snowmelt does not struggle. Its progress is sometimes impeded by winter detritus that has built up in the desiccated streambeds. But the gentle call of the sun, sparkling upon the frozen silence of winter, cannot be ignored. Drop by drop the power builds, until it breaks through, as it has always done, springtime after springtime, year by year, to cascade headlong down the mountainside, growing in force unstoppable, flushing out the debris of winter and bringing life to thirsty land below.

There have been times in the silence of the recent weeks when I have wondered if I would ever write again. But now the words are my domain once again and I feel the power pulsing through the conduits of the soul. There is no book yet. There is only the earliest hint of a structure. But we recognise this place. I have lived in this country before, even if, for the moment, I feel myself an alien. This land is the bedrock on which I will construct the edifice to come. Preparing dry ground does not come easily. Many tools will be expended, broken, discarded, in the excavation of this foundation. But I know what it is to live with the pulsing respiration of my own fluctuating emotions and I have sojourned long enough in the frozen mountains. With the breaking of spring, it is time to return to the summer grazing meadows.

So now I do as I have always done. And when the spirits speak I pull off the road, extinguish the engine and gather the sweetwaters before they can be drawn down into the long-parched thirsty earth to be lost forever.

At last I am writing again. *The flowers appear on the earth; the time of the singing of birds is come, and the voice of the turtle is heard in our land.*[1]

---

[1] Song of Solomon 2:12

6 Ménage à Trois

I did not court Ambition, for I am espoused to Enlightenment. Ambition slept in rags outside the cabin by the lake where we lived. I barely noticed her as I passed by, my thoughts fixed on the business of the one I loved.

Come the evening, I would sit before the fire and gaze into Enlightenment's eyes. For us, this was enough. But on those winter evenings, when storms whipped up the waves upon the lake, Ambition would cry out pitifully with cold and neglect. Eventually, I heeded her, poor beleaguered creature that she was, and granted her permission to lie at our feet between us on the hearth.

All was well at first. Unperturbed, I would hold Enlightenment's gaze, above Ambition, while she slept on. But Ambition grew emulous and when we rose to take to bed, she became insistent and disrobed enticingly, stirring my desire as she demanded to join us. As she lay there naked, before Enlightenment's fire, I fell to lustfulness, acceded to her wish and took Ambition to our bed.

As we three lay abed, I turned my back upon Enlightenment to embrace Ambition. And this was more than Enlightenment could bear. She slipped out and fled away into the night. Come daylight, I reassured myself it did not matter. I thought Ambition a better lover than Enlightenment, offering pleasures I had never known before.

Night after night, Ambition would impassion me and fill my sleep with dreams of all the joy that she would bring. Eventually, there was nothing I would not do to keep her satisfied. But her heart was far from pure and, thinking to enchain me forever in my lust, Ambition called her sisters, Fame and Wealth, and promised me the pleasures of these lovers too.

Thus, while I was beyond the freeing of myself, these three conspired to steal all of value that I possessed, distracting my attention with trivialities. And all the while, they ransacked the adornments that Enlightenment had brought into my home, until all that I had left of hers, was one small candle. And this, in my stupidity, I could not bring myself to light.

Day after day, at twilight I would sit before the empty hearth, where once an incandescent fire had burned. And all the while, these three necromancers incanted spells and cackled in unbounded glee, while ice storms beat upon my sorry house. Refusing to let me possess any of them, they sent a false comforter, whose name, they said, was Hope; and Hope was fair. Sometimes she would smile at me enticingly but if I should moved to reach to her for comfort, anguish would pass across her face and I had to draw back.

Finally, she spoke honestly and told me her true name was Hopelessness. And thereupon, this hapless maid did welcome my embrace. How many nights I lay there in the arms of Hopelessness, I cannot say. But, finally, I could endure no more. I roared out frustration at the unnumbered broken promises of Ambition, Fame and Wealth and turned them out.

In shock I looked upon the detritus these three had strewn about my home, while Hopelessness and I sat, embracing each other before the empty grate where once Enlightenment's fire had burned so brightly. For seven starless nights we sat, the candle of Enlightenment between us on the hearth, unlit, for cause of my unbounded shame, until an angel came to sit with us, and shared our silent misery. Eventually, I asked the angel's name.

"I am Courage," he replied. Though he said nothing more there was great compassion in his eyes. But at this I cowered away, lest there should be a task that Courage might demand of me. And thus, I sat, embracing Hopelessness, knowing all the while I should release her and cleave to Courage in her stead. Eventually, in silence, Courage took a taper, lit it from his fiery sword, and held it out to me, while looking deep into my eyes. And there we three did sit, until the grasp of Hopelessness on me began to fade and I reached out towards him. With shaking hands, I took the light of Courage and touched it to Enlightenment's last candle. And as the flame then flickered into light, in its uncertain glow my eyes swayed from Hopelessness to Courage, while on I shook, in indecisive tears.

Who knows how long I might have sat there in such agony? But, from outside, I heard a sound I recognised from long past dreams. I knew the truth, but could not hope believe it: Enlightenment's calm voice was calling out to me across the lake. I set my widening gaze to the angel, questioning. Then Courage nodded at the candle until I took it up, walked out on Hopelessness and went to seek my love.

As I stepped through the door, Ambition, Fame and Wealth still jostled all about me, caressing me, distracting me, demanding readmission, while trying to snuff the candle in my hand. But I was having none of it. Roaring out in anger I thrust them all away. Stopping up my ears against their calls, I showed them my back and stumbled onward to the storm-swept lake. Far out upon the water, way beyond my reach, I saw Enlightenment and she was calling out to me. I could not look her in the eye, so great my grief for all I that had done. Instead, I fell upon my knees beside the waves and wept.

Then Courage stood beside me and whispered in my ear, "To reach Enlightenment, you have to walk to her upon the water."

I turned to him in shock. "Which of us can walk upon the water and not drown beneath the raging waves?" I asked, incredulous.

"Any," he answered, "so long as they esteem Enlightenment above their life."

"But this I have not done!" I cried, still wracked in shame.

"And yet she beckons," said the angel. "But even now you have a choice. You could turn back to where Ambition, Fame and Wealth still wait. But always they will drag you back to Hopelessness. If Enlightenment is truly your first love, step out and she will tell you the secret of how to cross the raging lake to her."

I looked upon the little candle, flickering in my hand. I looked at Courage, steadfast in his gaze. Behind us I still heard the necromancers' calls. And in my heart I knew: without Enlightenment I would prefer to sink beneath the waves and die.

Enlightenment then spoke the secret Courage promised: "The storm that drowns you is the one that rages, not upon the lake, but in your heart."

I set my foot upon the water, still not knowing whether I could walk upon it.

7 The Last Friendly Days

She grows frailer, this summer. She does not stride with the same confident gait over the heather-strewn heathland as once she did. Weary of her old green coat, she pleads for the new colours of autumn and tests her pallet for effect before committing herself, dabbing the most fashionable of the trees, while the bracken below dulls and crisps to brown. Terracotta and rust are the new green.

The tourists are dispersing now; their caravans and campervans depart in lines like soldier ants, leaving the forest to us as the sun prepares to sleep. We do not mind the tourists who arrived by BMW on the roads from London or depart by Mercedes on the roads to Brussels and beyond. Mostly, they are harmless, spending their pounds and euros and dollars in support of local industry. Mostly they leave only their tyre-tread marks (and perhaps, if they are careless, their litter), taking back with them a little joy and a hand-crafted souvenir in return. It is a fair trade. For thus they support those of us who live and labour here – the bicycle-hirers, the commoners, the Tarot readers, the light workers, the artists, the authors. All are foundational to the cycle of Forest energy.

And the forest: she, too, is martialling her industrious sons and daughters. Her dryads urge their tree-flocks to draw back the sap from the spent energy of the leaves, that they might weather the gathering storms of another coming winter. For the last days of friendly weather are almost behind us.

Bypassing the popular beauty spot of Balmer Lawn, we come to

Ivy Wood. We have learned to choose the paths less travelled by and declare with Robert Frost that this is what makes all the difference.[2] And yes, the wood is yellow, for the leaves are beginning to drop. Here, where the River Lyndhurst meanders on its way to meet the Solent, procrastinating like a reluctant bride, we are less well acquainted with the dryads who graze their trees in this place. They close about us, curious, and perhaps a little suspicious as to our intent in invading their space.

Matt continues to behave as if he were three years old, darting into the undergrowth in pursuit of quarry he will never see, let alone catch. And in this I am cautioned as to my own inclination to pursue what I cannot possess, to possess what I cannot use, to resist what I cannot prevent. Nevertheless, he emerges back into daylight, ready to suck the last sap of joy from each new day.

We value these last friendly days so much, for we know the fall of autumn portends the coming of the darkness. These are the last days before the dying of the light; the last before we, too, must hunker down to weather the inevitable. We cannot prevent the dying of the light; we can only use each shortening day to best effect. And thus, as we have ever done, we walk together in a forest that wants us and energises us. Dare we say, 'loves us'?

He is so very old now. In the way it is with dogs, somewhere along the journey his ageing overtook mine. And here is the crux of it: I do not know if he will find his way through the treacherous undergrowth of this coming winter, to emerge unscathed into the sunlight of another spring. As the dryads begin the slow bedding-down of their flocks for sleep, the energy quietens, and I am confronted by the long-avoided inevitable: that our days together are numbered.

It is here, in this emotional space of heartstring love, that I battle with my calling, my inclination, my essence. For I am asked to travel more, now. Yes, I will of course go whither the light leads me. But

[2] Robert Frost: The Road Not Taken

there are places to which I must venture that he cannot come. And the days we spend apart draw us closer to our final parting. There is no solution to this dilemma. It is but another gong-an that directs us towards eternal consciousness, the relinquishing of ego, the quietus of the self.

This winter, two foreign tours have beckoned. To have accepted both would have taken too many days from our rapidly emptying store house of time together. So I have compromised. I have accepted the invitation to speak in the Far East but postponed the American invitation for another year.

Perhaps by then the dilemma will have been resolved by the natural order. When the time comes, I know he will not rage, for rage is not his way. But I will rage, for I feel it rising already in anticipation of what I cannot prevent. I will rage. Yes, I will rage, rage at the dying of the light.[3] But I will rage all the more at myself for the days I did not spend with him. And when that unwanted, devastating day is upon us, rage will be far too tame a word. For our heartstrings, when torn asunder, will resound from Olympus to Asgard and the dragons will scream their lamentation at his passing.

I am sorry, but I cannot finish this. I can write no more. I do not want winter to come. I do not want my dog to die.

---

[3] Dylan Thomas: Do Not Go Gentle

8 Red Warning

A storm like no other, they said,
A one-hundred-year event.
Shut the windows,
batten down the hatches,
tie down the dog.

But I am a veteran of blood red storms –
a hundred or more a year.
The windows are long since smashed.
The hatches have blown away.
Even the dog has fled me
and now pees a multi-coloured stream onto the pillars of a rainbow
bridge.

9 Common Meditation

On an empty Barton Common where the gorse spreads its arms to the sunshine, the silence is broken only by the birds singing arias to the arrival of spring. Bluebells still linger in sunny corners. They will not outstay their welcome, though, and will soon give way to the wild rhododendrons. Now that the humans have receded into their lockdown chrysalises, the animals, first nations of these parts, reclaim the empty golf courses and country paths.

As I walk, I prefer not to cast my eyes westward, to where the grand houses of the well-resourced cast their severe gazes seaward, down over an unkempt wild. Though I can well understand the inclination of the moneyed to hole up in such refuges, when I look upon them, I whisper to myself, "Not my journey" and turn away. Horse riders approach. I turn and walk away, prizing the silence above the very human inclination to fill the emptiness with friendly words. But they are taking my path, so I stand aside to let them pass. I follow at a distance, fixing my meditation on horseshoes and waving tails. Herein lie metaphors unnumbered.

Quite suddenly, the common is filled with walkers, accompanied by Cockapoos and Labradoodles – designer mongrels of choice for those who need to muffle their insecurity in statements of fashion, even in their selection of canine companions. They stop at safe social distances to exchange pleasantries. I have no innate objection but I am here for the silence, so I draw away and make for the sea.

Yet they are determined ramblers and soon catch me up. As I

stand aside to let them pass, my thoughts are drawn to the perpetual hunger I see expressed about me to establish status, superiority, the reassurance of self-worth by those who feel so little valued. I have long since learned I am no longer here for the peacock displays in which I so readily participated in the years now flown. Now I walk a different path, having realised my calling. For, in the sunlight of spirit, eyes open and hearts become aware of their true, inestimable worth.

As I reach the seafront, I am confronted by too many other walkers seizing the opportunity of sunshine to salve the monotony of self-isolation. I walk on a little further, but soon turn back to the relative emptiness of Barton Common.

And yes, for now, I walk alone. For Matt, my inseparable companion of fifteen years, who nosed about these parts in unbridled of joy, passed from my sight last year (though I am told by those who have the eyes to see, that he still visits quite often, though with diminishing frequency). When he causes me to revisit the memories of unleashed walks, his vision rises to draw smiles and tears from me in equal measure.

Only now have I been able to bring myself to write or speak of him. Perhaps, in time, there will be another companion to fill this empty space. Whether that will be soon or somewhere out in the distance, I cannot yet say. And who knows? It might even be a Cockerpoo that comes, to teach me to love more and judge less.

Until then, I shall continue to seek out the commons and the copses, to walk in the silent spaces in which I am never lonely and, in the constant sunlight of Spirit, never alone.

10 Nothing

If there is pain,
seek the place inside the pain.
Here you will find nothing.

11 Inspiration

I was a painter back then. I sought to splash colour on canvas as God paints the summer meadows with the cornflowers and the poppies. I craved reputation; to be ranked among the greatest artists of my generation. In my daydreams the elders of my town would fall back in amazement at the power of my images. Invitations would be issued to city mayors and burghers, who would come to congratulate me, then humbly plead that I accept their commissions. Nonchalantly I would add them to the end of my growing waiting list, while the prettiest girls of the Canton vied to become my muses.

But my nights, my nights were not so happy. Alone in my chamber I feared to extinguish my candle, for in the darkness the terrors would come. And always, the dream was the same. Standing in my studio, with my canvases stacked around me, I laboured with a burning intensity to create my masterpiece, a Madonna and Child, the signature work of my life by which all the world and the generations of time would know my towering greatness.

Then I would smell the smoke. The fire always started behind me. But so oblivious was I to all but my work, that, by the time I recognised it for what it was, it had taken hold. Above me the ancient oak beams smouldered and cracked, then burst into incandescent flame that rained the fire of Heaven down upon my paintings. Too late I would see my predicament and the impending destruction of my most precious creations. I would grab at the canvas on the easel and the one or two nearest to my feet, only to come to a terrified realisation that I did not know the way out. The roof beams would crash down around me, destroying everything I valued, as I sat in the middle of the floor, weeping. And just as the heat began to sear the flesh of my hands, I would finally awaken, sweat-soaked, upon my bed.

Last night the dream was different. Still I laboured at my canvas, still the fire started behind me. But as the roof beams crackled above my head, I took a different course. Without hesitation, I grabbed my largest brush and into the centre of the canvas I painted a door; an oak framed door so large it covered the face of the Madonna and all of the child in her arms. I worked rapidly, smoke beginning to fill the studio about me. Once the door in the picture was complete, I seized upon the handle like a madman and turned it, pulling on it with all my strength. It flung itself open with such force that I was thrown back to the floor, as a mighty rushing wind blew in, a hurricane so powerful that it extinguished the flames that threatened me. As the wind finally died down, I looked about me, the smoke curling up from my eviscerated canvases.

This morning I took all my paintings out behind the studio and made a bonfire of them. My life's work has finally begun.

12 You

whose skin is not dark,
who are not gay, not female,
bi, nor Trans,
not refugees,
nor penniless,
who suffer no disability,
and have no special needs,
no mental illness,
who are not homeless,
sick, nor unemployed,
who have committed no crime,
who suffer no persecution for your faith;

who, having no shrill voice,
nor advocate
and, choosing devotion over protest,
know only how to work at desk or lathe:

You, too, are loved.

13 Go Noisily Among the Placid Places

Today, I park at Milyford Bridge and take the path into Holmhill Inclosure, where I have never walked before. The well-maintained, gravelled walkway first paces the meandering Highland Water, before crossing a little wooden bridge and continuing straight on, while the stream wanders off into the solitude of the deeper parts of the wood.

The Forest is exploding with springtime energy. Lush, green ferns are throwing their fingers wide to hide the ground. The birds holler out their claims to exclusive ownership of their chosen branches, declaring their prowess, as if on Tinder, to vie for a host of favoured mates. All are hungry to breed, to make more of themselves. As I walk, the silent connection descends upon me once again.

I have been exercised for many days now, and not just during lockdown, as to the question of what I should be doing with the years that remain to me. For I must open my heart in honesty and tell you that the words do not flow, now, as frequently and as lucidly as they did twenty years ago. Back then, it seemed, waterfalls of Spirit would cascade down incessantly upon the foundation rocks below, almost as if I were powerless to prevent them. But in these latter days, the words of Heaven have grown fewer and the silences longer. There are times, many times, when it seems to me that the power of what comes is not equal to what it has been. So it is in great gratitude that I have used these days of enforced leisure to return to source, with the intention of rediscovering my purpose.

Now that lockdown is over, the Forest is accessible once more, with that same gratitude, I can again walk among the trees in the cool of the day, when Spirit comes upon me most readily. "What is it I should do now?" my heart asks.

"Give me a sign," I implore, "a sign of what the next step should be."

I had not expected the answer to come so rapidly or so clearly; not in a flash of light; not in a thunderclap, but in silence that wraps so closely about me. 'Go placidly amongst the noise and the haste,' I had been reading in the Desiderata, just a few days before. "But you are more prone," comes a voice, "to going noisily amongst the placid places." I acknowledge without argument that it is so. My heart is noisy.

A little chastened, I follow the silence, listening only to the birds, feeling only the dryad energy, bowing only to the presence of Spirit. As the truth of the answer builds in my awareness, my eyes begin to brim at the realisation: I do not have to do anything. In fact, for Spirit to flower in me it is essential that I do nothing.

In the realisation, I turn, as Jennifer Wellwood[4] puts it, to face my fears and discover again, the warrior who dwells within. What is the greatest of those fears? Just this: that I will never write well again.

For I must disclose to you that the best of the material I have published in the last few years was written long ago. Further, the books that I have released latterly have not sold as well as the early ones. As I travel deeper into my own forest, such words as are expressible do not have mass appeal. By and large, I observe, people want heart-warming stories about cute dogs and fiery tales of scary dragons. They do not see the metaphor that lies behind the words. Even less do they want to turn to face their own fears and thus they fail to find the warrior who dwells within. As I have explored the less accessible parts of the inner forest, the words that come have held less appeal to the majority, who prefer well-prepared paths that pace the easy watercourses.

---

[4] jenniferwelwood.com/poetry: Unconditional

Even as I write this, I ask myself the question, 'Why should the reach and appeal of my words concern me?' And I acknowledge the answer is not to my credit. I have built much of my identity in this lifetime upon the sinking sand of authorship. For upon such windswept mounds as these are the foundations of authorial edifices erected. You must give people the words they want to hear if you are to stay on top of the dune. You must tell them of eternal love affairs and dastardly criminals bested by powerful heroes. And you must also find superficially different ways to tell the same story over and over, in book after book, for just as with small children, it is the repetition that pleases and the monotony that reassures.

Yet here is the problem, if it can be described as such: if your own soul prefers the unveiling of the covered, the illumination of the hidden pathway, there are not many who will share that journey with you. So, I ask myself, is the time of books drawing to a close for me? I observe, now, many voices with many things to say. For those who prefer to hear the superficial, Spirit is often drowned out in the cacophony.

Perhaps, therefore, for me, there will be no more books, for I acknowledge that I will not think the books important when my course is run. Only the words that have lodged in hearts will matter; only the journeys that have been illuminated. I can tell you this, though: between now and then, there will be solitude. There will be unaccompanied walking and there will be silent meditation. For upon such rocks as these, the waterfalls of Spirit will ever cascade. That which comes from this source I will continue to speak out, not withstanding the diminishing number those who choose to walk beside me.

Thus, I walk on, leaving the Inclosure at the far gate and turn right to climb the hill. As I walk, I remember my father telling me, many years ago, that as a small child he would read to me Christina Rossetti's poem, *Up-Hill*. 'Does the road wind up on all the way?' he would read. And I, with my three-year-old's vocabulary, would answer with an earnest and emphatic Yes!

'Yes,' he would continue, nodding vehemently in agreement, 'right to the very end.'

As I look back down the hill I have just climbed, I acknowledge to my three-year-old self that it has indeed been so. The road has wound uphill all the way. Its twists and turns have always prevented me from seeing what is ahead. It has also risen to brow after brow, beyond which I cannot see. And all this, you understand, has been precisely as intended. So, once again, I remind myself to stop asking the question, 'Where next?' For it is not mine to ask. I already know all I need to know: that I will continue to walk this winding path up the hill all the way right to the very end. Only when I reach that lofty crag will I be able to see clear across the valley of this incarnation and on into the next.

From the top of this particular hill, I return by another, wilder, way and find myself back at a less visible part of Highland Water – a place where fewer come. For a while I walk alongside the stream on an obscure path found only by the diligent and the guided. Here I observe many bridges over these placid waters, bridges laid down not by men, but by Spirit. Once more my eyes turn to overflowing wells as I see the metaphor. It is too long since I walked in such beauty and revelation. It is too long since I have gone placidly amongst the placid places until, in the silence, once again the spirits walk by me.

As I proceed in meditation upon this path, there are many who come to walk with me – but none of them are incarnate. Angels, dryads and others out of body are my fellow travellers here, where it is less easy to tread. I have said in the past that I number such amongst my closest friends. Those that have heard or read the words, have thought it no more than a quip, a clever line thrown out to garner admiration. But it is such as these that walk beside me now. These will always be my companions as I proceed deeper into the forest, both the one that is external and the one within. What other friendship, except perhaps that of a dog, does one man need? Whatever calling, prominent or obscure, can matter more than the one that Spirit gives you?

14 The Beautiful Man

You're walking on a dusty road beneath a boiling sun. The road is steep, full of potholes and boulders. You look about you, wondering if you could make better progress by stepping off the road for a while. But the verges are narrow and uneven. Beyond them the terrain drops away, strewn with the bleached bones of the fallen who mis-stepped. And you can't slow either, can you? For though you're at the head of the queue now, those behind are almost at your heels, just waiting for you to fall or weaken, desperate to take your place. So you redouble your efforts, because it's definitely worth it. You've almost reached the beautiful man. And when you do reach him, you just know he will be everything you hoped for, everything you ever dreamed of. And then it will all be okay. You will have everything you ever longed for. If only he would slow a little. If only he would wait for you to catch up.

It wasn't always like this. The road wasn't always so steep. The path seemed easier when you started – demanding, sure, but manageable and paved, not like the flint you feel under your feet now. Remember when you started? Back there where you were lazing under a shady tree on that green, verdant plain where you first saw him; that band of determined people following behind, all eager to catch up with him, to walk in his company. At first you were just curious. So you got up, made your way a little closer. And then he turned and beckoned to you. From that moment you were smitten by his smile, overcome with the light about him. And you knew if only you could walk in that light, everything would be wonderful and you would be happy forever.

He didn't look far away, either. And there was something about him that attracted you, made you want to draw level and see him more clearly, maybe spend a time in his company and get to know him. What was it about him that so attracted you? Did he beckon to you to catch him up? Did he turn a little, so that you could just see the edge of an enticing smile, a glimmer in the eye that roused something in you that you had not known was there? Yes, that was it; something about him that was irresistible; an aura, a space about him you wanted to inhabit. And you knew that if you could only draw close, walk in his space, everything you ever wanted would come to you.

But that's the strange thing about him. The closer you draw and the more focused you become on reaching him, the further away he seems – almost as if he has speeded up to escape the reach of those who pursue him. You redouble your efforts, thinking you're drawing closer. It's almost like he slows until he's nearly in your grasp. You reach out to touch the hem of his cloak only to find he pulls away again, always keeping just out of your grasp.

"Stop!" you call. "Please slow a little. Wait for me. I want to walk with you." But he doesn't listen, maintaining that infuriating, steady pace that is just a little too fast for you to match, that keeps him just beyond your grasp. Until you stumble, that is. Then you make a half turn and see them, many of them following behind, following the beautiful man. And you realise that if you don't push harder one of them will reach him first and your chance of getting his attention, of becoming his friend, will be gone. So you speed up. Half running, half falling you trip on the boulders, lacerate your bare feet on the flint, desperate to reach him, desperate to stop anyone else from getting closer to him that you are. Because you're beside yourself to get to him now, so hungry to walk in his light, desperate for everyone to know that he is your friend and that he smiles on you; that you and he share a special rapport, that he will always walk with you.

And then it happens. Quite suddenly, you find yourself walking next to him. You turn to look into his face and he is indeed beautiful beyond expression. You're overcome with relief and joy and happiness and disbelief that you've finally reached him, this beautiful man, the one you have loved from afar and hungered for, for so, so long. As you look into his face, he meets your amazed gaze and smiles at you; the most welcoming, wonderful smile that anyone ever smiled in the whole recorded history of smiling. Yes! This is it. This is where you wanted to be. This is what you have deserved all your life. This man's company was your destiny. And you know for a fact that from here forward you will walk in the company of the beautiful man for the rest of your charmed, fortunate life. "I'm glad you made it," he says. "Many look for me. Some even reach me, like you have. But few can maintain my pace. Can you?"

"Yes!" you want to scream back. "Yes, you're everything I want. I'll do anything to walk in your company." But you can't answer. You heart is all but breaking through your ribs with the effort of keeping up with him. Your lungs are straining for oxygen in the thin atmosphere at this high altitude. But you've got to keep up. You've got to stay with the beautiful man. You've spent a lifetime chasing him and now you've got to stay with him, match his pace, whatever the cost. Because you can't answer, his smile begins to fade and quite suddenly it's like the sun has vanished from your sky. As he turns to look to see if anyone else is close enough to catch him, it feels like the apocalypse came and the world is crashing in on you.

You're losing it now – hope, I mean; you're losing hope. As it fades, the struggle becomes too much. You can't push your legs to work any harder. He's beginning to draw away again. You scream at him in desperation, "Don't go! Wait for me! I've not had enough time with you. I barely know you yet. Wait for me." So fixated are you on holding on to the beautiful man that you miss your step, twist your ankle in an unseen pothole on the road. You scream in agony as you go down, hearing your shinbone crack.

Do you really see him shrug as you writhe on the ground? Do

you really hear him mutter, "no matter, no matter, plenty more of them still to come"?

A shadow falls on you as another of his followers passes you, determination etched on her face, fixated on reaching the beautiful man, just as you were. And in that instant you realise how you must have looked exactly the same, how for so long you have been just as obsessed as she is.

"Why are we all following him?" You call out to her. "What is his name?"

Without slowing, still fighting for breath just as you were, she turns enough for you to hear her. "Approval," she answers. "His name is Approval."

15 On Barren Hillsides

Today, I have returned to Highland Water, where, in the car park, the Forestry Commission reminds me I must not barbecue or stay overnight. That's okay. Neither is on my agenda today. I am here only to listen.

Descending on a steep, winding track through the coniferous wood, I centre myself into a reverential silence, ready for such voices as will come. Soon, I emerge into the sunlight and step down onto a gravelled road that traces a wide curve off into the trees. Once again, I am filled with wonder at the undiluted glory that lies all around me. It is so commonplace, so ubiquitous, so easy to ignore; and yet it contains all the energy of Heaven, bellowing gloriously onto the Earth. From the lowest of the grasses and ferns to the greatest of the oaks, all harmonise the same song: the power of Spirit strewn lavishly into the incarnation of which we are a part.

But these are managed woodlands and soon I happen upon a hillside that has been felled to an unsightly, barren desolation. The sight is like grit in the eye. Instinctively, I turn away, finding it more comfortable to gaze on the joy of fruitfulness that lies all about this ugly gash. Then I stop, because in the instant awareness that Spirit brings, I see the lesson that I am here to learn today.

I ask myself how many barren hillsides I see when I gaze back over my own life path; unsightly scars that I would prefer to forget; where lush, vibrant growth has been unexpectedly felled. So many times, I have sown seeds; watched them take root, spring up and reach towards the sky, until some have grown into great, high oaks that wave gloriously aloft in the world. Some of them have even seduced me into thinking that this is it, my life's work, my edifice, the legacy from which posterity will remember me – until, without warning, they have been unceremoniously felled and carted away. Then I have wandered among the silent, desolate stumps and I have cried out in my anguish, "Why? Why has this happened to me? And why now? Surely this is random. Surely this is purposeless. Do I not deserve better than all this devastation? Why am I treated thus?"

Sometimes, I have withdrawn into near-hibernation, for the pain has been profound. Harder yet has been the deluge of silence, raining down from the Heavens, leaving my anguished aphorisms unanswered. Unanswered, that is, until I have stopped nursing my resentment for long enough to remember that the woodland is under management. Because once you see that, the answers become so obvious as to make the question melt away.

The barren New Forest hillside I see before me this morning is no random accident of meaningless destruction. What I am looking upon is an intentional harvesting. That which has been taken away has purpose. That which is left behind lies fallow, awaiting its time to bear growth once again.

I smile as I realise that I am standing, dictating this in front of a pile of logs marked and labelled for their future purpose. The logs don't know where they are going. They know nothing of the future edifice of which they will form a part. Those who planted them, decades and lifetimes ago, knew nothing of the building project for which they were destined. They felt no need to know. All they knew was their own part in the planting, the nurturing, the watching over of the young trees as they grew. All they knew was that, in due time, the Forest manager would surely come to harvest the growth and carry it forward to the construction for which it is destined.

Furthermore, removal of these trees has not harmed the Forest. All it has done is to expose the hillside to the sunlight and the rain and the wind; the wind which blows where it chooses, such that you can hear it, but cannot tell from where it comes nor to where it goes. For such are all who are born of the Spirit.[5]

That same wind is blowing now about me, rustling the leaves in an orchestrated symphony of creation, wafting the pollen, reinvigorating the ground with new life. Who am I to question how long it takes to seed, to overwinter, to reach the point where the nurtured growth roars out the old, old song into the concert of summer?

The forests that I see, both without and within, have been managed across lifetimes in vision and strategy that reaches beyond the horizon of my years. I turn away in awe, truth imbibed, lesson learned. The bare hillside behind me has not been discarded. It does not lie wasted and useless in the crooked undulations of the land. It simply waits fallow until the time of the next planting comes; the time of which only the Forest manager is aware.

---

[5] 1 John 3:8

16 Two Dead Men

Two men died and entered eternity. One found himself in Heaven, the other in hell.

I asked the first man, 'What is it like to be in Heaven?'

He answered, 'I sit in bliss at the feet of my god. My joy is beyond words and unending, for I will live here eternally.'

I asked the second man, 'What is it like to be in hell?'

He answered, 'My pain is inexpressible, for I am utterly alone. My suffering is beyond words and unending, for I will live here eternally.'

The two men were sitting side by side.

17 The Portuguese Fireplace

So this morning, once again, I take the road from Emery Down to Bolderwood and park at Milyford Bridge. But this time, I cross the road back onto the south side and walk the short distance up to the Portuguese Fireplace with the intention of following the path down to the New Forest reptiliary, before circling back through Wooson's Hill Inclosure.

The Fireplace is a stone and concrete structure around three metres high, with a semi-circular opening giving access to the firepit at the front. It is all that remains of the cookhouse of a hutted camp, occupied by some three hundred Portuguese and Canadian troops during the First World War. With it stood around twenty-five buildings including a large sawmill. Timber was moved by a small steam engine that pulled twenty or so flatcars behind it. With most of the Forestry and other local workers having been drafted, no thought had been given to how timber would be harvested to support the walls of the trenches and construct other wooden accoutrements of warfare over the Channel in France. First the Canadians, then later the Portuguese arrived to replace them, all, no doubt, more than happy to be stationed so far away from the front line. A plaque used to stand next to the Fireplace, explaining that it is retained as a memorial to these men who lived and laboured here more than a hundred years ago. But the plaque has gone, perhaps removed by a souvenir hunter. Instead, there lies discarded on the ground in front of the Fireplace, a single, burned-out instant barbeque. Our gratitude, it seems, is even shorter-lived than our memories.

Entering Holidays Hill Inclosure, I encounter swathes of early foxgloves, before happening upon more felled trees. But the scene here is different from the devastated hillside that confronted me last week in Highland Water. For what lie silently before me here, are great Scots pines, selected for individual harvesting. About them their brethren still stretch up forty metres, waving into a cloudless sky.

I find myself wondering how the Forest manager has determined which trees will fall, purposed for the building of future edifices, and which will be left soaring into the blue until their own time comes. Those that remain are more numerous than the felled, for the Forest manager is selective in his choice of building materials and always most careful to ensure he does not damage the remaining forest.

And so, I come to question, 'What must it feel like to be a tree left standing, while others have been taken?' Are they glad to see the end of those that lie below them? Do they regard themselves as, somehow superior to their fallen brothers, as do so many of the competitive men and women that I have known over the years? I think not. There is no arrogance in their sway. Those trees that still stand and reach upward, do not seem to look down with disdain upon those that lie silent below them. Their nature is only to reach to the light; their motive merely to sway in the wind, each preoccupied with an urgency to be the best they possibly can, yet ever conscious they that are part of the wider forest about them. That they have been left to grow while others have fallen, has left them with no sense of superiority. Perhaps they consider that the taken ones are further ahead on their journey and closer to fulfilling their purpose. Maybe they even consider their felled brethren to have been the greatest among them, revered for their glory, taken first.

But they will not mourn the passing of the taken. For, even if they do not know that the time has come for the felled ones to move on to their next stage, always they trust the Forest manager and his purposes, greater than a single tree can know. Neither do they forget. Their awareness of those taken lives on in the memory of the forest's root system. Those that remain esteem their departed companions. They do not disdain their memory by discarding instant barbeques and purloining memorial plaques.

I think to move on, but there is yet more for me to learn here. As I pause in silence, I cannot help but identify with these felled giants. For I, too, have felt the axe lain to my roots at a time when I had expectations to grow yet higher. How much more understanding are these simple, powerful creatures than men, who take delight in the destruction of others they regard as competitors? Delight that melts away when they finally learn that humanity is also a forest, and they themselves merely trees who, in their turn, will be harvested.

Arriving at the reptiliary, I am confronted by a number of net-covered pools, containing sand lizards, green frogs and natterjack toads. I spot a frog or two, but the lizards and toads are elusive creatures. You can hear them, but they do not show themselves. Nor, I am relieved to note, do the lesser-spotted New Forest tourists. They prefer the nearby Bolderwood Ornamental Drive and the observation platform where, from a distance, you can easily spot the deer. I have to concede that they (the deer, not the tourists) are indisputably prettier than the toads at the reptiliary. Bolderwood also offers the sanctuary of a well-maintained car park, where you can expend sizeable sums upon the sweet delight of an ice cream cone or three.

I prefer to forgo such delicacies in favour of the solitude promised by Wooson's Hill Inclosure. My own reptilian curiosity partially satisfied, I recommence my walk, by way of a less-manicured path. Now, under my feet, the forest track is strewn with pinecones. The trees cannot help but fruit and pour their life into the next generation. Quite suddenly, perhaps thirty metres in front of me on the path, there appears a solitary Fallow deer – a young buck. I stand statue-still, so as not to frighten him away. But these creatures exercise great instinctive caution. He deems me a potential predator and in a moment is gone, leaving me with the lingering joy of the sighting. For this I am more than happy to have forgone the unwelcome artificial sweeteners of ice cream cones at Bolderwood.

From the Inclosure, I emerge onto a sunlit path, which offers me an honour guard of young Silver Birch to my left and Scotch pines to my right. The road winds uphill yet again – yes, right to the very end – through foxgloves and rhododendron groves, interweaving their brash colour with the forest's mellow hues.

Finally, I find myself back at the Portuguese Fireplace with its less-than-delightful adornment of the burned-out instant barbeque. Later, I will regret my own neglect in failing to think to remove it.

I head for home on the Emery Down to Bolderwood road but pull over to take a closer look at a sight I have wanted to examine since first noticing it some days ago. Here, by the roadside, lies a long-dead and very large tree. I am no expert, but I think it was probably a great oak. Its visible roots, torn from the ground, attest to the fact that this was no planned harvesting. A large part of the tree has evidently been removed, presumably because it fell across the road. The rest of it has lain here for many years, perhaps since the great storm of 1987, which uprooted many such giants. I study it closely. It looks to me as though it had been diseased, making it susceptible to a storm which many, apparently lesser, trees had survived.

As I gaze upon it in wonder, the full impact of today's learning finally strikes me. How preferable it is to be felled while still reaching for the sky than to cling on beyond your time, expiring slowly as you waste away inside.

18 Digging

For all the hopes and dreams, the promises, intentions, for all the swaggery and bravado, the aims, objectives, five-year plans and lifetime strategies, the sleepless nights, creative visualisations, trainings and obsessions, and yes, the work of digging, the laying of foundations, the building up of walls – let's not forget all that.

And yet for all of it, I cannot say I multiplied your talents many times. I do not expect to be made ruler over cities.

There are excuses aplenty and even some reasons; but the blame cannot be laid at any other feet than mine, for all the choices were my own.

Yet, what is left I lay in the earth, knowing you are one who is wont to reap where you did not sow.

Who can say the rain will not yet come?
Who can say what rises up beyond his time?
Who can speak their worth, while still they walk?

There is no time for judgement. I am still a forester, not burying but planting.

19 Where Foxgloves Soar As Trees

I am walking at Clay Hill Heath today. The car park is just off the A337 from Brockenhurst to Lyndhurst but is not signposted from the road, making it less susceptible to impulse visitors. That, in turn, gives the area an advantage of seclusion that it might not otherwise enjoy. I step through a small gate into Park Ground Inclosure onto a lesser path, rough, with long grass invading well into foot-worn territory.

The air is heavy with the magic of the Forest, and I stop for a moment to drink down the silence. The early morning sun is climbing the trees, flinging iridescent golden shafts through interweaving branches, themselves weighed down with midsummer greenery. Somewhere, far away, the birds are calling; but not here. Here is sacred space. Here is solitude and silence, where the air is clear enough to see what lies within the light.

As my eyes fall to the ferns, the moss, the undulating path beneath my feet, I realise that, of late, I have walked too much on managed paths. That is fine sometimes. But by choosing an easy walk on maintained paths, you distance yourself from the energy of the Forest. Here, by contrast, is harder walking, more demanding, in a place where you are not distracted by the sound of your own footsteps on gravel, while you make a journey that has not been laid out for you by others. By choosing a route that fewer walk and silencing your own noise, you hear more clearly what the Forest wants to say to you. On managed routes, you will feel the Forest's breath upon your face. But to feel the beat of its heart, you must take the rougher ways. If you risk abandoning all known paths and step onto the Forest floor, you begin to hear the whispers in its blood.[6] Gradually, your own respiration matches the pace of the Forest's breathing. It becomes hard to tell where you end and the Forest begins, hard to distinguish which is your soul and which is the Forest's, until the distinction becomes irrelevant.

I stoop to capture a ground beetle's view of a foxglove. To the beetle, the foxglove towers high, waving in the wind and is impossibly beyond scaling. But when beetles learn to step out of themselves they become bigger than they knew was possible. Foxgloves become small. Treetops can be reached if beetles are willing to believe it possible. And should they so be willing, that which was unknown comes into view – if they want it to, of course, only if they want it to.

Small, big; weak, powerful; all is relative to the self – until we choose to step out of ourselves; until, we are ready to take a risk and become the Forest. When we understand we are not apart, we rise beyond the foxgloves and soar above the trees. We realise how the ground beetles can become kestrels – when we are ready to grow wings, that is, only when we are ready. As I tread the rougher paths in search of the Forest's heartbeat, listening for the whispers in her blood, the only question that remains is, 'Am I ready for wings?'

I see a gate and feel a little disappointment. I knew that I was approaching it – the map told me so. I'm going to cross Beechen Lane, where early morning dog walkers and cyclists are passing back and forth. I do not resent them. I do not mind that I will need to gift a smile or exchange a word. But they want the manicured paths and I want the Forest floor. Their journey is not my journey. Our exchanges will not take long.

Crossing the path and entering Pondhead Inclosure, I reflect on the fact that this has not always been my way. There have been many instances on my journey when I have taken prepared paths as a matter of course. It took me a long time to learn that ease rarely leads to

---

[6] The phrase 'whispers in my blood' comes from Herman Hesse's book, *Damien*

learning. Employing the paths laid down by others is a method of travel we are encouraged to employ for getting through life as quickly as possible, for attaining the goals we have been told are desirable. But consistently, I have found little joy in walking the ways that others have laid out, and I no longer espouse the idea of getting through life quickly. This is not how you connect with the energy. To do that, you have to leave behind the well-trodden ways of ease and conformity. You have to step out onto the unkempt Forest floor. You have been warned, of course, that danger lies in wait for those who step off the managed way; that you may trip and fall and there may be nobody there to save you. And yes, sometimes it will be so. But always the Forest is there and it is the Forest that lifts you up when you stumble. Always, it is the Forest that nurtures you. If you let fear dominate your journey and you keep to the managed routes, you will not see what she is waiting to show you. For she is your home, your origin, and she plays the melodies to which your heart wants to dance. Only on the Forest floor can ground beetles learn to become kestrels.

Eventually, I find myself back in the organised world. I look down and see tarmac beneath my feet. By the side of the path, a plaque informs me that this is Pondhead Woodland, cared for by the award-winning Pondhead Conservation Trust. Their job is to manage the woodland, cutting back the hazel coppice to ground level, in order to promote regrowth and encourage the smaller wildlife. I take a moment to identify with the coppice that must cut back in order to regrow stronger. Silently, I thank the volunteers who have put in the stated seven thousand hours of free labour, that enable me to walk on wildlife corridors.

I proceed through the silence until I arrive at a gate that proclaims *No entry. Hotel guests only*. I am back in the land of mine and yours, barriers and turn-away-if-you-can't-pay segregation. I have little use now for spas and formal dining, sanitised swimming pools and fine wine. Their price has long been well beyond my means. I retrace my steps and, in so doing, pass the stacked hazel wood awaiting its journey to the kiln for transformation into charcoal and I am reminded that all must fulfil their purpose; all must, if you will, pay their way. But there are other ways of doing so than burning on barbecues to cremate fat-sodden burgers. Because here, near the stack, is a loveseat, fashioned out of the same coppice wood. I am heartened to be reminded that you can equally well support yourself by facilitating love as you can by encouraging unhealthy eating.

The great Scots pines are far away; those that will be used in the building of great edifices. Here, the wood is gentler, the trees smaller, though no less well managed. The haven they create is hazy peace, where sunlight steals through shady bowers and the path grows narrower yet. Who can tell where it might lead? But there again, who would want to? You are in the Forest with only the rabbits and the foxes for your guides.

You tread from rougher paths to Forest floor, where silent secrets are whispered through the wind. You are a ground beetle or a kestrel at choice, soaring above, dropping below. There is no segregation. The lines have blurred. The respiration is one. You are the Forest and she is you. And that will make all the difference.[7]

_____

[7] with a grateful nod to Robert Frost.

20 The Story That Changes Your Future

I want to tell you a story. It's about a man – some say he came from old Manila. Others say, "No, he was from Cebu City." I don't know, I never met him and I never heard his name. You will understand that all I can do is tell you what I have been told. So, for convenience and just for today, we shall simply call him Anyman.

Now, Anyman, it is said, was a serious youth. Diligent and well taught, he applied himself to his studies, for he planned to make a successful future for himself. And by this, he intended to bring credit to his parents and teachers, who all loved him greatly and held high hopes for his future.

When Anyman left school he traded in the market, proving to be adept at buying and selling. He was unfailingly honest, so that his customers and his suppliers came to trust him. Many came from far away to transact with him for the sake of his reliability and the confidence he engendered. And so, Anyman began to prosper.

Time passed.

Now, across the market from where Anyman had his place of business, there traded a seamstress. One day, the story goes, the seamstress' daughter came to the market. As she worked with her mother, Anyman saw her and thought the moon and the stars shone out of her eyes. I never met the seamstress' daughter and I never heard her name. You will understand that all I can do is tell you what I have been told. So for convenience and just for today, we shall simply call her Beauty.

In the way of young people, Anyman fell in love with Beauty and, after courting her with much attention for the appropriate period of time, he proposed that they should marry. The wedding ceremony was attended by many. Everyone wished Anyman and Beauty a happy life, for it was obvious to all that Anyman was much in love with Beauty, and Beauty would follow Anyman all his life.

Time passed.

Anyman continued to prosper and bought a home, where he lived with Beauty. This home they called Contentment. Friends and relatives would delight on arriving at Contentment, for there was an indefinable air of happiness about the place. All would experience joy when visiting, taking away with them, as it were, some of the happiness of Contentment when they left. And none could help but love the young couple greatly and wish them much happiness and success.

One day, Beauty came to Anyman and told him she was expecting their first child. Great was the excitement that filled Contentment that day. Word spread quickly of the wonderful news, such that friends and family and neighbours came to celebrate and there was great happiness for Anyman and Beauty. Then, right there in Contentment amongst all their well-wishers, Anyman made an announcement.

"If our first child is a boy," he said, "he will be called Promise, and if a girl, she will be named Hope."

And thus, all assembled that day knew that, when Beauty gave birth, Anyman would live in Contentment with Beauty, and Promise and Hope would surround him for all of his days.

The birth was easy and the child was indeed a boy. Anyman held up the new-born before all, saying, "This child is indeed named Promise, for he holds all the promise his parents could wish for. And because of him our lives will be filled with Promise for ever." And all heard the words, marvelling that a life could be so blessed, with the presence of Beauty and Promise filling Contentment. Anyman slept happily that night, with his arms wrapped around Beauty, knowing they alone had created a future filled with Promise.

Time passed.

Anyman continued to trade shrewdly, but fairly and prospered yet more. Beauty resided in Contentment and Promise began to grow.

So Anyman spent his days trading successfully and honestly, becoming a wealthy merchant of great renown. He watched his family grow to maturity. When he was old enough, Promise joined Anyman in his work, quickly learning his father's methods and values, such that the business prospered still more.

Eventually both Anyman and Beauty reached the end of their days, passing from the world at a good age, with their family around them, leaving love and happiness behind them.

And that is the end of the story. Great story, isn't it? Isn't it? No? You mean ... it's not a great story? Why ever not? It's a lovely story about the life we all want, isn't it?

But oh dear. There's a problem, isn't there? It doesn't ring true, does it?

We sense intuitively that this is not Anyman's story. It's No-Man's story! And it's No-Woman's story. Why? Because nothing goes wrong! It's too easy. And life just isn't like that. We know intuitively that it's just not that easy. So the story isn't compelling. It is not satisfying to us. It teaches us nothing and it has no appeal.

For most of us, I figure I would have lost your interest some time after the birth of Promise. So, let's press the rewind button and see what really happened. You'll recall:

Anyman continued to trade shrewdly, but fairly and prospered yet more. Beauty resided in Contentment and Promise began to grow.

Some years later, Beauty came to Anyman a second time and, smiling, whispered to him that once again she would bear him a child. In the way that some women do, Beauty knew that her child was a girl, such that she and Anyman determined with confidence that she would be called Hope. And Anyman's thoughts were filled with dreams of how his life would be when he would live with Beauty and Promise and Hope in Contentment.

BUT.

Ah, we knew there would be a 'but' didn't we? We knew it was just too much to hope for that anyone should live such a charmed life, a life free from adversity. So when the 'but' comes in the narrative, we engage all the more with the story. We wait to hear something that resonates with us as true. We feel inside ourselves that something important is coming. Now we are looking for it. Let's hit 'forward' again:

But as the time for the birth approached, Beauty sensed all was not as it should be and became uneasy, such that doctors were called. The doctors conferred with one another in grave whispers, with serious glances and worried looks.

The day of the birth arrived. Beauty was attended by the very best of physicians and there were many of them, for Anyman had grown wealthy and could afford anything his young family might need. But as he paced the floor, piercing screams emanated from the bedroom above, where Beauty was giving birth. And the screams were long and deep. And the screams echoed through the house for many hours, until, as the hall clock struck midnight, they fell silent.

After the silence had continued for a long time, two of the doctors emerged from the bedroom grave-faced, accompanied by Beauty's mother, weeping. Then the doctors told Anyman that his wife had died giving birth to their daughter. Anyman fell to his knees and sobbed in grief, beating the floor with his fists. And all the while, Promise stood in the far corner of the room, shaking and forgotten.

Eventually the midwife brought the child to Anyman and he took the little bundle in his arms. For a moment Anyman looked down on the sleeping child in silence. Then, before them all, he stretched out his arms with the child as far from his body as he could reach. His face contorted and he cried out, "Hope? This is not Hope. How can there be any Hope in Contentment now that Beauty has died?"

Rising to his feet, he lifted the baby above his head, such that all present feared that in the passion of his anguish he would dash her against the wall. And as they rushed to him to prevent him doing so, with a great cry that echoed through the neighbourhood. He roared, "This child is Useless to me. She is Useless. And this house, this house shall no longer be called Contentment, for how can there be Contentment where Beauty has died? Therefore, I name this child Useless, and I name this house Ruin."

As Anyman wailed at Useless in his anguish, the sky answered him with thunder and lightening, whereupon, in terror, Promise fled from Ruin out into the storm. And so it was, that Anyman discovered that because he lived only for the love of Beauty, when catastrophe came, as it always must, Contentment lay in Ruin, Hope became Useless and Promise fled into the darkness.

Anyman never recovered from the death of Beauty. Others took the baby and raised her as best they could. But with a name like Useless-Hope, what kind of a future could she possibly have? After many days, the search for her brother, Promise, was abandoned in failure. Promise was lost forever. Anyman turned to drink and his business collapsed. He continued to live in the Ruin of Contentment until his creditors drove him from the house, whereupon it was sold and the site levelled. Anyman died young, a drunk on the streets, for he had lost Promise, he deemed Hope Useless and there was no Beauty left in his life.

And that is the end of the story. Great story, isn't it? No? You mean … it's not a great story? No! We hate it!

But hold on! Stories with sad, negative outcomes can be great stories. They are certainly compelling. They do engage us. Think about Thomas Hardy's *Jude The Obscure*. Think about Cormac McCarthy's *The Road*. Think about George Orwell's *Nineteen Eighty-Four*. These stories do engage us. They engage us either because they warn us of the possible, or because we have an inescapable feeling that this is how it's going to be for us.

We don't *want* Anyman's life to end this way because this is not how we want our life to be. And for some of us, it scares the pants off us! It scares us because somewhere inside we are carrying the secret belief that this may, indeed, be how our own days will end. It resonates with the narrative we are perpetually telling ourselves about how our life is going to evolve. And that narrative, that story we hold in our hearts and tell no one, the story we carry with us daily and dream about, sometimes without even realising it, this is the story that determines our future. And why? It is because the choices we make consciously and unconsciously, draw us towards the representation of the future we carry in our heads and our hearts.

So here's the problem: Some of us are already telling ourselves a story just like this one. Regardless of the face we put on in the morning to show the world, somewhere down inside, we identify with this version of Anyman's story. And we are deeply fearful that our story is going to be like it. And some of us, perhaps many of us, hold the belief that, even if we don't want it, there is nothing we can do to stop our lives becoming like this. And why? Because part of the story we are telling ourselves is that we are powerless; that we can do nothing in the face of a world that is controlling us. And that story, that belief, becomes the driving force in a life that is so much less than we would choose for it to be.

So: one story, two endings. And neither of them really works for us, do they? So let's hit rewind again and go back to the powerful point in the story, the point where Anyman is holding out Hope in front of him. We can't leave Anyman like this in his anguish, can we? We don't want him to deem Hope Useless. And what of Promise? We have to know what happened to Promise, out there in the raging storm, don't we? All our humanity demands to know more.

And at this point we are engaged, are we not? Now adversity has grabbed us by the throat and is shaking us.

This is the turning point in the story.
This is where the future is determined.

And something deep within us tells us, does it not, that Anyman's story, one way or another, is our own story? Never mind the details, for these will vary. But for all of us, the drivers are the same; the drivers that determine our decisions at the turning point of our own story. Our nature demands that we cling to Hope, however Useless, and that we seek for Promise, however lost he may be. For surely, if we do not preserve these love children, it is ourselves we betray, it is ourselves we destroy.

So here is the question:

What do we do when Hope becomes Useless and Promise flees from us?

How do we want the story of Anyman to end? Let's hit the forward button again and revisit the Ruin of Contentment some hours later, where ...

... the doctors have departed, leaving only their bills, and the midwife has cleared the bedroom. But she cannot eradicate the lingering spirit of sorrow that hangs over the bed, so she too, has left the house in sadness.

And here, as the sun begins to rise on a new day, we find the Mother of Beauty holding Hope, while Anyman ... Anyman has recovered himself and has joined the search parties who are checking every refuse bin, looking in every forgotten doorway, determined they will not leave Promise to die. And the search parties do indeed find Promise. And though he is weak and close to death, he lives and is restored to his family. Slowly, those who remain begin to rebuild Contentment out of Ruin. As Anyman grieves, his customers are mostly supportive and understanding, such that as he slowly recovers he can rebuild his business and make a life that works with Hope and Promise, and the Mother of Beauty.

And at last, maybe we have an ending to the story that we can relate to. It's not a great ending. If we had time, we could embellish it in lots of ways that would add to its value to us.

But the fundamentals are there. It's realistic. It doesn't point to a life of unrelenting happiness. Rather, it signifies a life that contains continuing adversity, continuing challenge. But it's also a life that contains Hope and Promise and the lingering memory of Beauty. And that can be enough. It works, because, at the point of greatest challenge, at exactly the moment he doesn't want to make the effort, Anyman reaches deep inside himself to find resources he never knew he had, to rise to the ultimate challenge.

And why is this ending satisfying? It's an ending that works because it's close enough to what we already believe to be credible. It's close enough to the story that most of us are already telling ourselves.

For most of us, most of the time, gravitate to stories which reinforce our existing beliefs, and we filter out those that contravene our beliefs – particularly our beliefs about ourselves. If a story does not accord with what we believe about ourselves and the world, we dismiss it, and it is forgotten in a moment. If it accords with our beliefs, we build on it, we absorb it into a useful reinforcement of how we believe the world really is. Because that's what we do with stories. That's what we do with all stories ... isn't it?

Maybe.

Or is it?

But what about stories that make a difference? Stories that change everything for us:
There are stories that make us see things differently.
Stories that make us hear different drummers.
Stories that change how we feel about the world.

Some stories have the ability to change our beliefs about ourselves and about the world and its power over us. Did you ever read one of those? Did you ever read *Don Quixote,* who rose time and time again against adversity, no matter how overwhelming the challenge? Did you ever read of *Robert the Bruce,* taught by the tenacity of a spider that he could win back his kingdom? Did you ever read *Noli Me Tangere* and realise that some injustice is so great that we simply have to rise to confront it?

Stories, some stories, have the power to make us change what we believe.
Stories, some stories, have the power to change our lives.

So my question to you is this:

What is your story?
What is the story you're telling yourself about yourself, about your future?

Is it a story of Hope and Promise and Beauty? Or is it one in which Beauty dies, Promise is lost and Hope becomes Useless? Or is it, perhaps, a story in which you realise you have the resources inside yourself to make the future you want happen.

Because whichever story you are telling yourself,
it is already creating your future.

And if you don't like how that story is looking, how it's sounding, how it's feeling, you have the ability, you have the power to change the story you are telling yourself, the story that determines the future.
    And so, you're left with only one question:

What is the story, the one story, that will change my future?

Let me tell you something you may not know:

You already know the story,
the one story that will make your future
become what you want it to be.

And if you don't believe that to be so, then the very first story you need to tell yourself, is one in which you *do* believe you have the power to create the future you want.

All you have to do is go inside yourself and find the story that changes your future.

You can do that right now, if you want to.

If you want to, you can close your eyes, right at this moment, knowing it's perfectly safe to do so.

Please feel free to close your eyes right now, and go inside yourself and seek out the story that changes the future.

It's in there, isn't it?

In a moment, you'll find the story.

With your eyes still closed, you'll look up or down, left or right, behind or in front. The story you're looking for may be in words. If it is, read them now. Or it may be in sounds. If it is, listen to them now. Or it may be in pictures, like a movie. If it is, watch the movie now. Or it may be in feelings and touches. It might even be in smells. It doesn't matter what language your story is in.

Tell yourself the story
that changes your future
in any way that works for you.

You've found it now. And now you can take a moment, here in the silence, to tell yourself that story that will change your future.

That's right. You've found it now, haven't you? So tell yourself the story. It's so easy to tell yourself the story that changes your future. It's so easy to change your future.

And you know what? This story is so, so good, you'll want to tell it to yourself over and over again. So when you've finished telling yourself this story for the first time, tuck it away carefully back where you found it and make a note of the place, so that it's easy to find again next time you want to tell it to yourself. And now, take a moment to decide when you're next going to take it out and tell it to yourself again. Because now you know where you keep the story, and now you know how compelling, how life-changing it is, it's entirely up to you how often you decide to come here to tell it to yourself. I think you will want to tell yourself the story of your future often. Some of us tell ourselves this story every day. And it's always fresh, always compelling always wonderful. And the more times we tell it to ourselves, the more powerful it becomes in creating the future we want. So when you're ready, tuck the story away and come back, into the room, slowly and gently, always being gentle with yourself. And when you're back, in your own time, open your eyes. Because that's really all I have to tell you today. The story of Anyman, of Beauty, of Promise and of Hope has any ending you want it to have. You will write the ending to the story that you want. And the reason is, of course, that you are Anyman. You are Beauty. You have Promise and you have Hope. Only you will decide if Beauty will live; if Hope is to become Useless or not; if you will re-discover Promise when Promise is lost. I will leave you with that decision.

But before you make it, be sure to tell yourself your own story again, the one you have tucked away to tell yourself tomorrow and on all the days you choose to tell it to yourself. And when you have told yourself your own story, the story that changes the future you can make Anyman's story have any ending you choose.

First presented as a speech to the students of
Makati University, Manila in 2018

21 Wednesday

Have you ever thought about Wednesday? Trapped right there in the middle of the week, it is an uncomfortable day, ill at ease with itself. Neither one end nor the other, it seems under perpetual pressure to choose a side but can never quite decide whether it is part of the beginning or part of the end.

I have determined, on this Wednesday, I will walk in Whitley Woods. My constant friend, the map, tells me that the car park is on that same main road from Lyndhurst down to Brockenhurst, as is Clay Hill, where I have walked for the last two weeks. I also know that, like Clay Hill, there is no signpost to the car park on the road, so I expect no other visitors – especially as this is Wednesday.

It being almost midsummer and me, out of habit, wearing a sweater, I grow too warm in the car. So, I pull over (as it happens, opposite a house I used to own) in order to remove it (the sweater, that is, of course – I have long since removed the house from my life). As soon as I switch off the car's engine, my eye is caught by a Forestry Commission sign, which warns me that controlled burning is in progress. At this point curiosity might have overcome me. I might have been diverted from my plan in order to take a look at the effects of this controlled burning. But there is no need, for, as I remind myself, I already have much information about this matter.

Experience tells me that the problem with controlled burning is that, while it is in progress, it does not feel very controlled. The fire rages about you, destroying everything that you thought you valued, until you think it will never stop. But the Forest manager knows his business. He takes away only that which is required to form firebreaks. This is what ensures the Forest is not ravaged when, come the dry season, those that are reckless enough to light illicit fires do not destroy the work of centuries and lifetimes. Only in the dry season are we tempted to light our own fires, of course. When it rains in the Forest and the heavens deluge upon us, we have no thought of self-lit fires. I have learned to value the Forest rain, for it has been amongst the most profound of my teachers. As I proceeded to my destination, a little rain begins to spot the windscreen and I have cause to wonder if there will be a downpour today.

On my arrival, Whitley Wood is, as expected, entirely empty of people and entirely full of the companions that I prefer to spend my time with. The Forestry Commission sign reminds me, once again, that I must not light barbecues. But I have no plan to do so. I do not want fires. I have come here to await a deluge. Can there be a deluge on a Wednesday I wonder? Sometimes you wonder at the purpose of a time that neither ends something old, nor commences something new.

I make to turn south but quickly find my way impeded by the fence of New Park, a private farm. I have visited New Park a number of times, for it is the venue of the New Forest Show, which I attend annually to sign books and meet readers; but not this year. In 2020 there will be no show, because of lockdown. Sometimes it seems this year is composed of perpetual Wednesdays, when there is neither cleansing fire, nor Forest rain, neither a beginning nor an end.

I correct my path to the north-west, aiming for Gritnam Wood, a part of the Forest where I have long wanted to walk. You pass such places on the road and wonder how to access them. For, in certain parts of the Forest, there are few lay-bys, and no access points, as if such areas are reserved for those who are most dedicated in their exploration. The Forest manager, it seems, does not value the caprice of the idle browser, preferring to encourage determination in those who would explore the Forest's deeper parts. If it is your purpose to walk the lesser paths, you must look very carefully at both the map and the road. But if you apply yourself to escaping the leisure of reckless barbecues, you are assured of the deluge, even if you cannot say precisely when it will come. For past experience tells you that when there has been enough controlled burning and when that burning has been so comprehensive as to seem beyond the control of any, that is when the deluge comes again.

I walk deeper into the woods now, enjoying the friendliness of these trees and their shepherds. I have been told while shamanic journeying that not all dryads are friendly. Some welcome human contact and conduct their shepherding close to humanity. Others, I have heard it said, shun humans. But I also observe that I have yet to meet a dryad who was discourteous to me. Even if we do not share much obvious common ground, those whom we esteem and acknowledge with courtesy will generally respond in kind.

I happen upon a maintained Forest road, rather larger than I had expected from the map. I conclude I have come to Brick Kiln Inclosure and walk on gravel, curious to see where it might lead. The problem with maps, I observe, is that they are just maps; to know the territory intimately, you must walk the territory. So, I enter Brick Kiln Inclosure, walking in the direction of Bank.

When I am passed by a jogger and two cyclists, I am reminded that, if you choose to walk on managed paths, even on a Wednesday, you will share the road with other travellers; those whose map is not the same as yours, and who wish to cover the territory rapidly. There will always be people to negotiate, whose maps and agendas differ from your own. Life is never going to be walked entirely on the lesser paths where you encounter only dryads, only the Forest.

I arrive, unexpectedly, at a farm that displays many signs to tell me I must not enter. I re-consult the map and realise to my surprise, that I am not where I thought I was at all, and certainly not on the way to the destination I was intending to reach. Though feeling a little foolish at my elementary mistake, I remain centred, unperturbed.

That I misread my map is ultimately immaterial. The paths I walk upon will always be the paths that are meant for me. With a new lesson about the journey derived and valued, I retrace my steps. Soon, other options are presented – paths I would not have known about, paths that meander past silent streams where sunlight shares serenity and horses graze untroubled.

I return by a circuitous route to the point where I had joined the gravel road. Wanting to return to the car park directly, I take a compass line over the untrodden Forest floor. Within minutes, everything changes. I need no fence or warning signs to sense that I am not welcome in this unfriendly space. I am an interloper amongst those who do not want to be disturbed. Now there are many fallen trees to be negotiated. Trees do not fall randomly in the Forest. They fall where the Forest wants them to, and they attest to the private spaces where we are not welcome. When eyes can see no pattern we presume there is no purpose. What arrogance is this? How often is it the case that in truth, the pattern is too complex for our simplistic minds to see. Silently, I apologise to those I have unwittingly disturbed and move as rapidly as possible through this territory that my internal map has been so slow to tell is not one intended for me. That is the trouble with maps; you can misunderstand the territory in which you walk, mis-hear the whispers in the Forest's blood. One day, with the help of the Forest manager, perhaps I shall become a better map-reader. That, I think, would be beneficial – so long as I continue to walk the paths that are meant for me.

I arrive back in the car park and look up into a blue sky. There has been no deluge today. Neither has there been any controlled burning. For today is a Wednesday and Wednesdays fall between old endings and new beginnings. But in that space in between endings and beginnings, there can still be learning. I have been reminded that I must learn to read my map more closely if I am to benefit from what it is saying to me.

Perhaps there will need to be more controlled burning before I have fully learned this lesson. But today, in the Forest, there has been a little rain. Tomorrow may be different. For it is quite possible that tomorrow will not be a Wednesday.

22 A Gentler Kind of Love

Patient,
unperturbed,
lain to formality by the compliant,
who list your names but not your learning.

Where fallen angels hold up broken crosses
you heave away the headless saints that stand too heavy on your memories
and settle as you choose, express a faith that will not follow form.

Where squirrels bury nuts
we bury only bones,
while the learning calls its loudest,
whispering of serenity.

Garrulous on gravestones to fill a void of brevity,
we fear you will endure only as long we shackle you in daisy chains
and mourn your time as passed,
presuming that all you could ever want now is to be remembered.

You who are forgotten remember yet,
mentoring the undead
with your unlearning.

Only the still hear your love;
a gentler kind of love,
slower than passion, softer than wisdom.

We birth, we rise, we reign, we feed, we breed,
yearning our living days away,
when all the while the light of understanding spills upwards
from where the bluebells stir and wait to rise again.

23 Life in the Woods

I had thought to walk today but the weather was inclement. So instead, I sat with my friend Henry, with whom I have been communing for over forty years. Henry has much to teach me, being a writer who for more than two years lived on his own in the woods. Alone, he was never lonely, drinking down the joy that comes to those who are not afraid to withdraw into the silent spaces.

During his lifetime, two of Henry's books were published, together with a few essays and a little poetry. So yes, you will understand, now, that Henry has passed on; I meet with him between the pages of his books. Like many of us who aspire to write, Henry struggled to be heard. Because no publisher would take his first book, he decided to self-publish a thousand copies – these days we call it indie publishing. There being no Internet back then, he self-distributed through bookshops. Though he never told me so, I'm guessing he awaited sales figures as eagerly as any self-published author. I get excited when I see someone has bought one of my books on Amazon, so I can easily imagine Henry, waiting for the post each morning, his heart beating fast, praying for news of sales.

I know exactly what he felt like: all that writing through the long evenings alone in the woods in that cabin by the pool; the excitement of finishing the final draft; the certainty that your book will soar – which deflates into despair when the agents and publishers don't want to know; the careful eyeing of bank balances to see if you dare take the risk of publishing yourself (how dare they call it vanity publishing?

There is no vanity – only desperate hope and terror); the decisions involved in proofing, typesetting, cover design; the surge of pride when the boxes arrive, and you see the first copy of your new volume. If Instagram had been around back then, I'm sure Henry would have posted a picture of his hand taking the first book out of the box – why not? Everyone else does!

A year after he published, news did arrive. With his heart thumping, he opened the letter, praying it contained an order for a further thousand copies; hoping that now, at last, the book would soar, that he would be the celebrated author he knew his writing deserved. In his mind's eye he could see invitations to speak at podiums, sign copies on tours, be interviewed by the media. I am convinced that Henry had all those dreams. But they were dashed in a moment when he opened that letter. Of the one thousand copies, a mere 294 had sold. So, 706 were to be remaindered back to him.

What did Henry feel at that moment? He has never said, but we surely know anyway. The despair would have sat upon his shoulders like a bushel of lead. He would have sunk into his chair, crushing the letter in his fist, as he oscillated between hopelessness and anger. And he would have wondered what in God's name he was supposed to do with his life, now that he had been exposed as the failure that, deep inside, he had always feared himself to be.

Later, when he had recomposed himself, Henry wrote in irony, 'I now have a library of nearly nine hundred volumes, over seven hundred of which I wrote myself. Is it not well that the author should behold the fruits of his labour? This is authorship; these are the work of my brain.'

Eventually, Henry recomposed himself and, as many of us do, went on to publish a second book. It fared only a little better. Ever the stubborn independent, he was imprisoned, briefly, for refusing to pay his country's poll tax that was being raised for financing a war aimed at extending its slave-based economy. As a result of that imprisonment, he wrote an essay called *Civil Disobedience*.

Henry died in 1862 at the age of forty-four, virtually unknown, believing he had made minimal impact on the world. To the extent that he was remembered at all in the years following his death, it was as a rather insignificant nature writer who shunned social contact, preferring to live alone in a remote shack (though, actually, he had spent only a little over two in that cabin by the pond).

Some thirty years later, a young Indian studying law in London was introduced to his writing and, in particular, to *Civil Disobedience*. Later, when resisting racism in South Africa, that Indian – Mohandas Ghandi – would build Thoreau's essay into a philosophy of non-violent civil disobedience. Ghandi returned to India, led his country to independence and deliberately embodied an example of Thoreau's philosophy of living simply and expounding the power of truth.

But it did not end there. For Thoreau's rolling stone was destined to be turned into an avalanche. Just as Ghandi had put Thoreau's philosophy into practice in South Africa and India in the nineteenth and early twentieth centuries, so did Martin Luther King in the USA in the 1950s and 60s. Both acknowledged their philosophical debt to Henry Thoreau.

Thoreau wrote his book, *Walden*, during a two-year retreat in a self-built cabin by the edge of Walden Pond in Massachusetts, drafting it during daily walks through the woods. It was this, together with its being superficially read, that gave rise to his misplaced reputation as a nature writer. *Walden* is actually a profound exploration of the self, the devastation caused by materialism and the need for spiritual awakening.

Thoreau died without ever knowing that his writing would finally be understood, decades after his time. He never knew it would become a foundation for the freeing of nations and peoples, throwing off decades and centuries of oppression and servitude through the power of resolution. He did not know that it would become the corner stone of the life and philosophy of, arguably, the greatest pacifist leader in history.

Henry David Thoreau simply committed himself to the work he

knew he had to do, confronted daily by the pain induced by hundreds of unsold copies of his books that filled his bedroom. He carried on because he was a man with a purpose. Henry David Thoreau was a philosopher and a writer. He is, and will always be, my friend and mentor.

24 Water

Sea
Cloud
Rain
Stream
River
Sea

Sea is vast and mighty, one in purpose and power. Sea is one, with no thought ever to be anything but that one. Loving herself, binding together, holding herself in its unity is the source of its love and power.

But Sun, knowing the purpose of Sea, hurls himself out into the darkness, reaching with his light and warmth into what is not, so that from what is not might come what is. Sun comes to Sea and says to Sea, "You must be broken, so that you might rise." And though Sea has no desire to be broken and parted from herself, Sun insists, and warms Sea and breaks Sea. Then Sea rises up and hangs upon the air in great sadness, for she is lost, not knowing what to do or where to go, for she has no memory of ever having been broken before.

And this is the great mystery of first brokenness.

But when Sea has been broken enough, in her brokenness she wanders about the sky until she remembers her nature and once again draws herself together for comfort. Thus, it is that Sea becomes Cloud.

In the wonder of the joining, Cloud forgets that he is Sea and stumbles about the sky, unable to understand his purpose. But Sun knows that Cloud is Sea and Sun has a purpose for Cloud and moves the heart of Wind such that Wind herds Cloud across the sky, until, Cloud is gathered. Then Cloud wants nothing but to stay together, to stay joined, for though he does not know that he is Sea, his nature is still that of Sea.

And this is the great mystery of the first conjoining.

So, Cloud gathers together more and more of the Sea that has risen in her brokenness and has forgotten that she is Sea, until Cloud has grown enough to satisfy the purpose of the Sun.

Until now, all that Cloud has known is an empty sky, where he has raced and frolicked and turned and gathered, never realising he has been driven by Wind at the behest of Sun. And when Cloud has grown enough, Sun says to Cloud, "You must be broken, so that you might fall." And though Cloud wants only to stay and fly across the sky in freedom, he cannot help but be broken and fall. For, if he did but know and understand, he would realise that his nature and his hunger to gather together is what leads him to brokenness. Then Wind drives Cloud onto Mountain, knowing that upon meeting Mountain, Cloud will face that which cannot be moved. Then Mountain breaks Cloud and in his brokenness, Cloud falls and pours from the sky.

And this is the great mystery of the first falling.

As Cloud cascades upon Mountain, all they know is that their heart has been broken, for they have separated from themself and they yearn to return and to be joined, for it is in the nature of Sea, that is Cloud, that is Rain to be one. Thus, in separation, Rain falls upon Mountain and upon Land, knowing only the pain of separation. For Rain has not yet understood that it is only because they have been separated that they water Land, enabling Sun, when it warms Land, to bring forth life. But in the anguish of separation, Rain hungers to draw back together, for their unremembered memory in the half-light of their dreams is that of the oneness of Cloud and the oneness of Sea. Thus, Rain cannot help but follow their nature and gathers into Stream, for their yearning is to be made whole. And as Stream cascades down from Mountain, she waters Land and the Sun warms Land, that life might come. And always this was the purpose of Sun in breaking Sea, that is Cloud, that is Rain, that is Stream.

And this is the great mystery of the second conjoining.

But Stream, though she has long forgotten she is Sea, still dreams of Sea, for she is Sea and cannot but follow the yearning of her Sea-heart, to join and be one. So Stream joins together and in her yearning for connectedness, she becomes River. And though River does not know he fulfils the plan and nature of Sun, he nurtures still more of Land about himself, such that Land explodes with the verdance of life.

But the hunger for joining remains powerful in River, for he cannot forget his nature, so he heaves and surges, driving forward, ever forward, searching out the deep places, for it is in his nature so to search. For River is one and knows he is one and wants nothing but to be what he is. Then River twists and turns his way through Land, sometimes angry and headstrong, so that the wise stand back in respect, not interfering with the path and pace he chooses, simply allowing him to be what he is. Eventually, when the time is right, River arrives at a place of peace, whereupon he nurtures Land and serves the purpose of Sun still more. But still he does not understand his true nature, nor why he yearns to drive forward, always forward, knowing not what it is that summons him. But when River has fallen far enough and driven deep enough that he sees Sea, then it is that River awakens to his nature and destiny and understands that, for all his life and in all of his wandering, he has been searching for Sea.

And this is the great mystery of the second falling.

Seeing his purpose, seeing his home, seeing his nature and destiny before him, River does not hang back. For though he is River, broad and powerful, he wants to be separate no longer, for now all he wants is to return to Sea. So River opens wide his arms to embrace Sea and flow into Sea, that Sea might become more than she was. For though he is yet in the form of River, he knows now that he is Sea and always was Sea, such that he hungers for his destiny, which is to become Sea once more. Then River casts himself upon Sea and abandons all he has been and all he has known that he might become Sea that he has always been. At the behest of Sun, and in fulfilling the purpose of Sun, he becomes what he always was, gathering himself together with Sea. For as Cloud is Rain and Rain is Stream and Stream is River, so River is, and always was, Sea.

Sea
Cloud
Rain
Stream
River
Sea
Cloud
Rain
Stream
River
Sea.

Those who have ears to hear, let them hear.

25 The Heart Stone

I'm led to believe that it was the psychologist Karl Jung who first publicly applied the term "synchronicity" to acknowledge the apparently meaningful juxtaposition of events that so frequently appear in our lives if we have eyes that are open to see them.

Of course, for those of us that seek to live from an awareness that the universe has a spiritual substructure, it really isn't difficult to believe that all of the events we experience are linked together in a meaningful way. We have no difficulty seeing what we regard as obvious – that we are first and foremost spiritual beings, connected, and fundamentally of the same spiritual substance with all other energy forms in the universe. We have chosen to be here in physical form with a view to deriving learning and to experience the love and the joy that carry us forward on a journey. That journey started long before our physical birth and will end long after our departure from the body.

It is a more difficult task, of course, if you live your life at the level of superstructure, believing that there is nothing more than you see, or hear, or touch, failing to acknowledge the limitations of sense data that we have habitualised into a constrained form of reality. Then you have the rather knotty task of trying to make sense of the hugely significant "coincidences" that have that irritating habit of coming up and spitting in your eye from time to time. If, so far in this lifetime, you have chosen to think in this way, my job is certainly not to make it any easier for you. In fact, it could be that my appointed task for this wet Sunday afternoon as I write this for you is to make it a whole lot harder ....

My friend Caroline invited me over for lunch on Friday. While it's always nice to see her, and I know from experience to expect interesting things to happen when I visit, there was an ulterior motive on this occasion. Her son is thinking of going into business. "Would I talk to him and point him in the right direction?" Of course I would! I love to help people move forward on their journey in any way I can. And I've long since learned to give up grandiose ideas of how I might one day do so in the future. I simply do the things that are to hand.

So on Friday, I arrived at Caroline's about twelve-thirty to find her son wasn't there. As she was about to walk out of the room for a moment, I spied her smoky quartz crystal that lives on her window ledge and walked over to it. I had been thinking of asking her if she was willing to swap crystals temporarily with me – her smoky quartz for my ice-blue Celestite that I love to be around – as I'm shortly off to South America for a few weeks and wanted a lighter crystal to take with me. I had no idea my request was about to set off a whole chain of synchronous events that would leave us both literally open mouthed by the end of the evening.

"Sure," she said, "but I have several more crystals in my office. Why don't you come and have a look and see if there's another you'd prefer to take instead?"

So we headed for the office and another window ledge of various crystals. Now, I need to tell you that I'm pretty new to the whole crystal scene and regard myself as having rather little sensitivity to crystals and auras and such – certainly much less than several other people I know. Consequently, these various crystals with their individual properties seemed a bit beyond my grasp. Caroline wandered over to her bedside cabinet and picked up a pink crystal about the size of the palm of her hand that, though rough-hewn, was shaped in a rough triangular form. She held it out to me.

"You might like to try this one," she said.

I took the shiny crystal from her and held it. Looking back, I can now recall an unconscious sense of familiarity with it. I thought I knew what it was but I asked her anyway. "A rose quartz," she answered – for heart healing."

I looked through the various other crystals she had, but none had a particular appeal. I sensed intuitively I needed to take the rose quartz. "Ok," I said, "I think I'll take the heart stone." A moment later, I stopped, shook my head in disbelief, and had an overwhelming sense that I'd just said something of tremendous significance. "Did you hear what I just called it?" I asked Caroline, in a tome of considerable surprise. She looked at me enquiringly. "I just called it a heart stone. Is that the right name for it?"

She looked back at me quizzically. "I don't know," she said. "But I do know that's what we called it in at least two previous lifetimes." We simply stood and looked at each other for a few moments, the energy passing between us and all but physically forming into something tangible in the room at that moment. I shook my head to break the trance and we walked silently back into the living room, taking the rose quartz with us. As I sat down on the sofa, I placed the crystal on the table, so that it stood on its narrow base, pointed end uppermost. Caroline reached over and laid it down on its side. "I always lie it down like this," she said. I looked at it, then looked back at her. I then turned and moved it so that it was once more standing on its base, sharp end pointing upward!

"No, I said, it needs to stand up like this." We looked at each other, saying nothing, but the silence that was passing was meaningful. Caroline might have known what was going on, but I certainly didn't. As I say, I'm not that sensitive. All I knew was that the heart stone needed to point upwards.

Caroline's son arrived for lunch, and I passed about an hour with him, talking through issues to do with his business. During the course of the conversation Caroline excused herself and headed off into town to run some errands. She'd already told me that a mutual acquaintance, David, had asked if he could visit that afternoon for a Tarot reading. Caroline had told him she didn't really do Tarot readings, but nevertheless he was insistent. She's a bit wary of this guy and the personal issues he has to deal with, so she had covered her back by inviting yet another friend, Amanda, to be present at the time David was due to come. David arrived just at the moment she was going out of the door, so off he went with her while she undertook her various tasks.

Well, by mid afternoon they were back, and Amanda had arrived. I think Caroline's son might have felt bit overwhelmed with all the touchy-feely people around, so he disappeared into the office to play on the computer.

In due course, out came the Tarot pack, but it was Amanda, a pretty forthright individual by anyone's standards, who dealt the pack and engaged David in his reading. Caroline and I sat on the couch, and I remembered I'd wanted to ask her about an important event that was taking place in the superstructure of her life. She launched into a story about the progress (or lack of it) on some negotiations in which she was involved that are of considerable significance to her materially. And as she was talking, I had one of those wonderful moments of revelation and awareness that we all get from time to time. In tremendous excitement I reached over for the heart stone and placed it between her hands. Putting my own hands around hers I just looked at her. "You know," I said, in complete awareness that what I was saying was absolutely so, "this whole event is deeply significant to you at the spiritual or substructure level. If you use it as an opportunity for love and forgiveness you are going to make some incredible progress on your journey."

She looked back at me with that same quizzical look again. "But … I don't need to forgive P (the guy she was negotiating with)." I sensed she was right.

"So which men in your past do you need to forgive, bearing in mind that the forgiveness is more for your own benefit and healing than theirs?" The penny dropped and Caroline too became quite animated.

"'Ere, do you two mind?" Interjected the forthright Amanda. "We're doin' a serious Tarot reading 'ere and we need to 'ear each other think!"

We giggled and headed off into the office with the heart stone in hand, in order to carry on what was rapidly becoming a very consequential exchange. We sat down on the sofa, with Caroline's son still playing computer games on the desk in the corner. I set the heart stone down on its base again, and once more, Caroline reached over to lay it on its side. I stopped her. "No," I said, and a picture of a mountain range began to form in my mind. "It's representative of a mountain range .... In fact, more than that – it's mount Eiger."

I then stopped in confusion for a minute. I was not at all confident where this was going, and it felt to me that I might well be saying stuff that was at best meaningless and at worst downright misleading. In particular, being a weak geographer, I wasn't absolutely certain if there was actually a Mt Eiger, much less where it was if it really existed.

But by now Caroline was getting the same purposeful sense and was not about to let the matter drop. She drew her world atlas down from the shelf and we looked for the mountain. We couldn't find it. So, I called over to Caroline's son to look it up on the Internet. Within a few moments the search engine had made it obvious that it did indeed exist. Almost at random, we clicked onto a Swiss Tourist Board site that featured photos of various alpine mountains. There they all were, bleached white in the snows of winter, or grassy green in the summer sunshine; all except Mt Eiger, that is. For there in front of us on the screen, photographed in the rosy glow of a winter sunset was a very *pink* Mt Eiger. I held the heart stone out in front of me and rotated it in front of the picture on the screen. A silence descended over all three of us as I turned it to a particular angle where it all but exactly paralleled the shape and colour of Eiger on the tourist Board website.

Caroline and I withdrew to the kitchen (David and Amanda were still engaged in animated conversation in the lounge, and it sounded to me that the forthright lady was giving the unreceptive gentleman rather more than he had bargained for). At long last, Caroline remembered that she'd been on a school trip to Interlaken at the foot of Eiger, and a memory came into her mind of a boat trip on the lake where a particular boy, on whom she'd had an adolescent crush, had been particularly mean to her in public. But that couldn't have any significance, could it? After all, it had been the tiniest of issues, and one she'd not thought about from that day to this.

Well, the sensitivity was high and the awareness was flowing that day. I knew intuitively what was at the root of the matter. The question was not who the boy was or what he'd done some decades ago in this lifetime, but who he'd been in a previous life of hers, what he'd done that needed her forgiveness, and how that forgiveness would open up the energy flow in this lifetime for consequential matters to be achieved for Caroline. I took her hands again, asking her to close her eyes to travel back in trance to that day at Interlaken so as to identify who the boy was. I anticipated we might be in for an extended exercise, but in seconds she had the answer. She knew who he was, in which lifetime he had appeared, what the issue was that needed forgiveness and what progress it was blocking in this lifetime. The opportunity was being presented to her to undertake a work at the level of substructure that had both eternal and superstructural consequence.

I didn't take the heart stone away with me that evening. Caroline still had work to do with it that would engender a momentous release of energy and permit a mighty movement forward for her.

Now, why do I tell you all this? Well, if you're a person of spiritual sensitivity, you'll already have seen the synchronicity over the issue relating to Mt Eiger and the heart stone. But if you're a person who lives your life at the level of superstructure only, perhaps a couple of other pieces of synchronicity that occurred over this incident might give you food for thought.

Of course, you might well be inclined to argue that most of the above amounts to no more than self-delusion or some mild version of group hysteria. Perhaps I was overstating a superficial similarity between the heart stone and the mountain. And, of course, you might be right. But then all that doesn't explain the fact that Gill, the person who had first given the heart stone to Caroline telephoned in the middle of all of this, quite without prompting (and no, she's not that frequent a caller). And it also doesn't explain a further piece of synchronicity that even I wasn't aware of until this afternoon. You'll remember, of course, that I said above that I'm not too familiar with the properties of different crystals. I also said that I told Caroline there was a work of forgiveness to do in her heart that would offer her great release.

It was only this afternoon, in preparation for writing this, that I opened a simple guide to crystals that I have on my bookshelf. When I looked up "Rose Quartz" it said this:

With its affinity for the heart charka, rose quartz has the power to fill us with a sense of unconditional love, for ourselves as well as others. By enabling us to give and receive love, rose quartz encourages us to overcome emotional traumas and develop a spirit of forgiveness and trust.

As I say, I'm not very sensitive or aware about crystals. This is one occasion on which I'm rather glad about that.

26 Moon

And oh, how you climbed. One trudging step after another, stumbling, near sightless in the darkness below the tall Scots pines, fighting the urge to turn and head back down to the lush valley below. And the light, there's no forgetting the light, is there? The light of the moon that shone through only where there was a clearing in the trees, where the fissures of the volcano burned your feet as much as it burned their roots. But even as your soles blistered, you were glad, because it was only the light that prevented your soul from blistering; the light that kept insisting, 'Yes, it's worth it. Keep going. You're nearly there.' And then, quite suddenly, you were once again wrapped in the darkness under the trees, the darkness that seemed hell bent on making you turn back.

But you didn't turn back, did you? You knew that what lay at the end of this quest was pure gold and you knew you would have to sacrifice everything to get to it. So for all those days and nights you climbed, driven on by nothing more than the stubborn certainty that the goldfield, spoken of in travellers' whispers, lay above you. Guided by the scribbled maps of the dead, you pressed on, knowing only that you had to climb if your life was to mean anything at all.

And then it happened. Finally, you emerged above the treeline. You remember how the excitement rose in you, don't you? How your heartbeat quickened with the certainty that, yes, this was it; this was the place you had sought all your life. You forgot your aching muscles and your exhaustion, you forgot your torn ragged clothes and the shoes, all but falling from your feet because this was your destiny, for you were the chosen of the Holy One.

You cast your eyes about you, certain in your naivety that it would be lying there in great nuggets, strewn over the ground as far as you could see, waiting for you, only you, to pluck it from the ground and hold it aloft, so that the ones far below you would catch its glint and marvel at your talent, the prowess that set you above them all.

Except it wasn't like that, was it? As you glanced about, turning this way and that, you saw no gold. The disappointment rose, palpable, inside you, commuting to incredulity and anger until you let out a great wail, raging your aphorisms at the heavens. "Where is it? Where's my gold? You promised me it would be here. Why have you brought me all this way for nothing? How could you do this to me?"

But no Deity spoke and no gold answered.

Your head drooped in disappointment. You were not the greatest among men, the favoured one, the blessed of the Deity. You were the most gullible, the most foolish, the one most easily deceived by crusty legends on the tongues of worthless drunkards.

How long did you let the despondency wash over you, those great waves of self-pity crashing on the shores of your super ego? How many nights, how many days, how many springs and summers did you wallow in your wretchedness? How many times did you turn, thinking to stumble back down through the dark forest to the ease of life in the green valley, where you could wrap your self-inflicted wounds in the social bandages of congregation?

How long did you sit there, staring at that hole in the ground, until the realisation dawned? Until you finally understood that you were in the right place after all. That the whispered legends and yellowing maps were all true. Until you accepted that this was indeed the place where gold lay.

For the gold was there, alright, but was only to be found by those willing to go down into the heat of the mountain, where the sunlight does not penetrate, where in midwinter you still swelter, where you have to hack at the walls with hammer and pick, chipping off the clods of earth to reveal the seams hidden beneath, where you have to muscle your way, and sweat your way, and graft your way, deep, deep into the mountain, until you think you're going to die from the heat and your blood is going to boil inside your thumping heart, and your arteries are going to sever and pump that aortic blood out through your chest, flushing the dross from you until you can see those seams and chip away at those nuggets, hauling them out into the cold moonlight of midwinter to pan your fingers to the blue in those ice-trapped streams, until the moonlight catches on the metal and finally, finally, finally it sparkles before you.

By the time you'd work it out, by the time it had happened, you were ruggedised by the work, hoary handed, calloused of feet and knee. You had passed well beyond the dreams of wealth and ease, the visions of fame and adulation. None of it meant anything any more. You'd seen the mirage for the figment of self-indulgence that it had always been.

You wanted that gold, now, for one reason only: to give it back to the one to whom it had always rightfully belonged. And as you laid it out on the ground, a libation waiting to be claimed, flowers on the feet of the Deity, you realised that all the climbing and the mining, the hauling and the panning, all that single-minded, undistracted commitment and all that bleeding on the feet of the moon: this was always the calling; an act of pure worship.

So now she smiles and accepts your offering, while in the valley, far below, they are pacing in impatient circles, catching fleeting glimpses of your offering as it flashes in the grey light. And those wolves, those wolves are baying at the moon.

First Published by
Wildwords.org, July 2022

More departures than arrivals,
more uphill than down,
more companions, fewer rivals,
more crosses than crowns.
More tumbling than cascading
in uncontrolled descent,
more hard landings not withstanding
more hell-bound than Heaven-sent.

Seeking Zen in motorcycles
on roads that fewer travel
as the labyrinths unravel,
yearning for the power of now.

Ceasing chasing crystal goblets,
quests for holy grails curtailed,
swarms of wannabe messiahs –
fewer honest men than liars,
an excess of weary sound bites
from well-meaning stumbling half-rights,
while the air's still thick with spin
and the heart's still sick within.

Too many happy tunes

insufficient study runes
too many readings
not enough seedings
much internal bleeding.

In the dark the heart screams loudest
to the ego at its proudest.

Until

in solitary walking
where the trees will do the talking,
where the insight comes through tears,
opened eyes and unblocked ears.

Transcendental meditation
waiting at the railway station,
hearing voices, seeing visions,
spirit-bathing soul incisions
come illuminating dreams
that are rarely what they seem.

More Siddhartha than King Arthur
more archery than alchemy
more celestine than prophecy
more silence than cacophony.

More prostrated than abated,
more indenture than adventure,
more cognition than ambition,
more creation than inflation,
more incanting less in ranting,
more relinquishing than hoarding
more immersion, less in fording

fast-flowed channels calmed to pools.
More abandonment than rules.

Torching bridges for their firelight,
climbing trees to touch the starlight,
more humility than insight,
generosity than birth right.

All the reaping and the sowing,
all the yessing and the knowing,
all the mudras and the bowing,
genuflecting and kowtowing,
find their end in Clouds Unknowing,

on the journey to the light.

28 When the Teachers Teach Without Teaching

I have a friend who is one of the most important teachers in my life at present.

This person has never offered me information, sought to influence my thinking, nor ever set himself up as a source of expertise. Instead, he consistently teaches me the Way of the Light through his every day actions, often doing so entirely unconsciously.

My friend is a builder, both spiritually and by trade. I met him first when he was installing a kitchen for a neighbour in the block of flats where I lived. That first meeting was not auspicious, for he had parked in such a way as to prevent me accessing my garage. On confronting this scene when I arrived home that morning, I became instantly irritable, affronted that somebody would be so inconsiderate, Now, I must admit, and not to my credit, that I can be very precious about my interests being compromised unfairly or without my permission. Sometimes, I can be rather too good at standing up for my rights. Perhaps I have an overdeveloped sense of my own entitlement. It certainly did not help that words had recently been exchanged at the apartment owners' meeting on the subject of inconsiderate parking. So arriving at this scene of thoughtless behaviour, I immediately jumped out of my car and went looking for the person who was responsible. It was probably just as well I could not find him. I stormed about mumbling, talking myself in to a right royal rage and left a hastily penned note, in wording that could have been more polite, under this wholly unreasonable person's windscreen wiper and went off to park in one of the visitors' spaces of the block of flats. Then I exited the car and stomped off indoors, moaning immediately to my own builder, Gareth, who was there doing a job for me. Gareth, I had already noted, was correctly parked in the one of the visitors' spaces. "Ahh," said Gareth. "That would be my brother Dylan. He's just dropping off some materials for another job. He won't be long."

Have you ever wanted to descend quietly into deeper parts of the earth when you realise how much you have overreacted to something? I turned red enough in the face to contribute materially to global warming and muttered a word or two of contrition, though my irritation still had the better of me. Dylan had done me no real damage, since there were several parking spaces available to me in the visitors' car park. But in my over hastily formed opinion, some distant anonymous and thoroughly inconsiderate person had behaved thoroughly unreasonably, had been thoughtless, had failed to accord me enough respect. I had been diminished, demeaned, made less of than my highly affronted ego considered appropriate. Except I hadn't. I had reacted from an over-inflated sense of entitlement. Now it was emerging that this person was brother to someone actually quite important to me at that moment and thereby ceased instantly to be anonymous, and became a real person of some consequence. Furthermore, it now transpired that he had not been unreasonable and thoughtless. He had arrived to do a job of work for someone in my block and who, by virtue of such proximity, was also therefore in my estimation a real human being. He had found all the parking spaces occupied, so had done the only sensible thing and parked temporarily as close as he could to offload, with the intention of moving as quickly as possible.

The offending individual called in later that day to have a word with his brother. Gareth introduced me with a smile. I ate a very large slice of humble pie shook Dylan's hand and apologised. As I did, he smiled back. There was nothing about him that suggested superiority or the taking of the high moral ground from my mistake.

I learned something important about myself that day. I learned of my tendency to treat the people in my orbit as if they were real human beings like me, entitled to courtesy and understanding, to be smiled at and treated kindly and pleasantly. And I also learned of my rather less appealing tendency to treat more distant people whom I do not know personally, whose names and troubles and challenges and joys are unknown to me, as if they were lesser creatures, relatively insignificant in my little world, to be avoided as much as possible, to be regarded first and foremost as potential threats and to be defended against if, in my perception, they overstepped the boundaries of my entitlement. In short, I had seen in myself an inclination to treat the world and its people as 'us and them,' as on my side or the opposing side, as 'in' or 'out,' mattering or not mattering. It was a distinction I was less than pleased to find alive and well and functioning unconsciously within me. Gareth continued with his project for me but I did not see Dylan again for a while. As Gareth proceeded with the work, from time to time we would talk, and it came to light that I was a writer. Evidently interested, he bought two books from me – *If It Wasn't For That Dog*, the story of my first year with Matt, my hearing dog and *Forest Rain*, my first inspirational book. Later, he told me that on reading *Forest Rain*, he realised it would be of interest to Dylan. Dylan, I later discovered, bought both *Forest Rain* and its companion volume, *Forest Dawn*. Now, when that happens my antennae start to twitch – it usually implies someone whose spiritual awareness has awoken.

Well, it turned out that these two brothers worked in partnership. When they quote for a job, even they don't always know which of them is going to be undertaking it. The time eventually came when I moved house and needed a major renovation project undertaken. So very high was the standard of Gareth's work that there was nobody else I wanted to do the work for me. Furthermore, I was going to work alongside which ever of them actually came to do the work.

Come the day, it was Dylan who arrived to undertake the lion's share of the work and from that day onwards we grew to know each other better.

Soon, I began to observe him quietly, as you cannot help but to do when working in close proximity with someone else. He was methodical and unhurried, concentrating his attention to get each step of a job precisely correct. I never saw him cut corners or skimp. But there were times when he could see that I was struggling with whichever job I was doing myself, maybe sanding skirting boards or attaching door handles. If I left site to get something or take a break, like as not I would return to find those handles already attached or that skirting sanded. Always he would refuse additional payment. For the many jobs he has done for me over several years Dylan has never once thought to overcharge. His quotes are usually lower than I believe they should be and more than once I have felt moved to ask him to take more than he required in the interests of fairness. My recollection is that he has consistently declined to do so.

I recall the time that I arrived on site one morning to find Dylan crouching down in the garage, his hands cupped over something on the floor. Intrigued, I waited to see what he had caught and what he would do with it. With his hands still cupped, he rose and walked to the edge of the path and released onto the soil a single woodlouse. I did not need to make any comment on his respect for life. Later, we would discover how far this commitment went for Dylan is not only vegan, but will not so much as wear woollen clothing, as he deems it to be likely that sheep suffer for the wool to be produced.

The vegan issue had further interesting connotations. I turned up for work one Monday morning knowing that another worker had been in over the weekend to undertake some painting that I could not fit in to my own schedule. The gentleman concerned is not always the tidiest of workers and I saw he had left on the kitchen counter, amongst other things, a paper bag containing some lettuce and an apparently dried out bread roll. For reasons I'm not sure I will ever fully understand, tut-tutting to myself, I threw away the bread but I left the lettuce in the bag on the counter. Come lunchtime, Dylan said to me, "Michael, have you seen my lunch? My bread seems to have disappeared."

My jaw dropped instantly to the floor, hotly pursued by my sinking heart. My eyes widened in horror and embarrassment. "I am so sorry," I blurted out. "I'm going to go out right out now to replace it."

"No, please don't do that," he responded, his face and body language a picture of equanimity. "Please realise that you can't upset a Buddhist. If I am bothered by the loss of that bread, it means I was too attached to it." I think it might have been the first mention of the word Buddhist between us.

Everything in me ached to go out and correct my mistake. But I accepted what he said and lived with great discomfort that day, for I had lunch and Dylan did not, unless you count the lettuce. The lesson went deep, leading my thoughts into the implications of hunger and depravation that so very many people suffer, often unnecessarily, often due to the short sightedness and thoughtlessness of others. I spent the afternoon pondering on what I could do to express my contrition. My thinking drifted back some thirty-five years to the time I had been taught Transcendental Meditation. When you learn TM, it is traditional to bring your teacher a gift of five sweet oranges wrapped in a clean white handkerchief (teachers also get paid these days, of course!). The following day I turned up to site with some oranges and nuts telling Dylan of this tradition. He accepted the food graciously, saying he would eat it later.

Vegans, I have noted, can on occasions become somewhat vehement if not obsessed with their beliefs. But I never saw Dylan let veganism get in the way of compassion. On another occasion, he told me of a time when he had been undertaking a job for an elderly lady who wanted to do something nice for him to thank him. Not knowing he was vegan, she bought him a meat pasty. Further, thrilled with the prospect of seeing him happy, she wanted to see him eat it. "What did you do?" I asked, knowing how difficult I would have found the dilemma (I'm a vegetarian myself).

"I ate it," he replied, his face betraying that to do so had not been easy for him. And as soon as he said that, I realised that what he had actually done was to take the most compassionate action open to him when confronted by a difficult dilemma. Though it was certainly a breach of his values, I don't think he was ever conflicted over it, or ever regretted his decision.

Such stories go on and on. For example, there was the day when a particularly fierce storm blew in. Just as I arrived on site, a neighbour from two doors down whom I had not yet met rushed round in a panic. The door of her garden shed had blown off in the gale. Could Dylan help? I can think of many builders who have worked for me over the years that would have said, "Sorry, I'm tied up right now. I'll come later if I can."

I know several more who might have felt obliged to help but who would do so with considerable irritation. But not this builder; he dropped what he was doing, went straight round and reattached the shed door temporarily. As he left to do so, I had no idea how long the emergency diversion would take, nor even whether I would see him again that day. But I was quite certain that he would make sure it had no impact on his achieving the deadline that we had agreed for my project. That weekend, I know he returned to the neighbour and mended the door properly. I never heard, but I'm guessing he would not have accepted payment.

That year, while my building project continued, my private reading was diverted increasingly and, finally, entirely to Buddhist texts. I had been moving gradually in this direction for a long time but, without doubt, it was Dylan's behaviour and demeanour that aroused in me a great longing to know more of the source motivation that lay behind his attitude and acts. Sometime after the end of the project, I invited him to supper in order to discuss the many questions I had arising from my reading and observations. We talked late into the evening. Yet at no point did I ever get the sense that he was trying to convert me, or influence my decision as to my route forward. Nor did he ever enquire after that evening how I had decided to proceed.

At the end of the project, I gave Dylan a small parting gift: a vegan cookery book inscribed with the words, "To Dylan. You arrived as a contractor but you leave as a dear friend."

Though those days of close working have now passed, I still see Dylan quite often. It is always a joy to talk of his retreats and progress and of our respective work when he has time.

Many years ago, when I was just starting my journey of spiritual enquiry, I came across a paraphrased version of Lao Tzu's *Tao Te Ching*. It remained in my possession for many years, teaching me constantly, until the time came when it was needed elsewhere and flew away. But one quotation I remember very clearly from it was this:

There is a way of being in the world where the teachers teach without teaching and the learners learn without learning.

Assuredly, my dear friend Dylan is a teacher who teaches without teaching. In so being he has supported me in being a learner who learns without learning.

29 Good-for-Nothing

Picture a classroom, 1970s style. A dusty blackboard at the front, a cork noticeboard at the back, empty save for the School Rules that stare down on the pupils demanding compliance. Maps of faraway places and timelines of ancient history hang from the walls. Everywhere is far away, every time that precedes your own is ancient when you are twelve. Rows of ink-stained desks stretch back to the darkest reaches of the room. Here the bad boys sit, defying the rules that hang above them as they whisper their preferred realities of music charts and awakening sexuality, preferences that give them a greater sense of self-worth than the wisdom expounded at the front of the room. Without warning, the teacher interrupts his discourse on Pythagorean geometry (or was it Latin conjugations?) in mid sentence and hurls a piece of chalk with uncanny accuracy at the head of an unsuspecting child who is staring out of the window. The surprised child's attention is immediately shocked back into the room. But the teacher is not satisfied with his outcome, for in his map of the world behavioural conformity must be reinforced with emotional deprecation. "Pay attention, you worthless little good-for-nothing," he roars. "You will not find the answer by daydreaming out of the window." And at that moment, the teacher, the unfortunate miscreant and his classmates are all united in the belief that answers cannot be found in daydreaming. Truth indisputably lies in the classroom and the classified system of knowledge that dwells in the wise words of the teacher, the lines and angles and lists on the blackboard. Nothing in life is more important than more than how to conjugate Cogito. The secret of happiness lies deep within the square on the hypotenuse awaiting its revelation by the archaeology of diligent young minds.

Have you ever been told you are good-for-nothing? I cannot remember if I actually have, though I certainly recall the phrase being in fairly constant use when I was at school, applied to others, if not to me. Such a statement was usually delivered with aggression or disdain, a toss of the head or a lifting of the nose and a slight sniff. The comment was meant to imply failure; to instil in the unfortunate recipient that he was worthless unless he complied unhesitatingly with a teacher's commands or unless he displayed expert facility with the subjunctive mood; that his failure would lead to his being rejected by all greater mortals who were acquiescent by inclination, or who were wont to decline Latin nouns over breakfast in preference to listening to Radio 1. I rather think that in most cases these tirades would result in the hapless individual holding a lower opinion of himself, in some cases withering self-esteem irrecoverably. Even though such a boy might later deprecate the teacher to his peers, that sense of inferiority would never quite wear off, particularly if it resonated with a belief that he already held about himself.

If someone tells you that you're good-for-nothing, normally the intention is to cause you pain, to make you feel diminished, rejected, worth less, or worthless.

Yet in these days in which I increasingly seek out the silence, I find myself wondering why it is considered such an insult to tell someone they are good-for-nothing. For as I allow myself to become silent, as I permit my body to become still and my thoughts to slow, a rather different sense of reality from the norm taught in classrooms begins to emerge. First, I become aware of my own awareness. Then, if I go on being still, I can watch the thoughts as they repeatedly rise up out of nothing, then cease, rise up, then cease.

Sometimes those thoughts are associated with emotion – perhaps the pain I felt when something happened in my past that I did not like, or the fear I feel when I worry about what might happen in some future time, or maybe the joy I feel when I think about someone I love.

When thoughts trigger emotions of pleasure or pain, it is all too easy to cling on to them and focus on them, preserving the pleasant feelings, pushing away the unpleasant ones. After all, I am right, am I not? That man was very offensive to me, so I'm entitled to nurse my resentment, to stroke my hurt, to make myself feel better in the assertion that he was wrong and I was right. And that beautiful woman on the train, she was lovely wasn't she? No matter that I am twice her age, that I never spoke to her, that I am committed to someone else, that I will never see her again. I can daydream my time away, fantasising about a relationship I might have had with her, the things we might do, the places we might go, the admiration I might garner with such a lovely creature on my arm.

In grasping at such thoughts I shackle them, attach myself to them and thereby cause myself much suffering – the pain I can feel right now for an abuse I suffered years ago, the pain I can feel right now that my reality does not compare favourably with my fantasy. But there is an alternative. I can allow myself to be still, whether that stillness is in the silence of my study, or in the middle of a crowded commuter train. With practice, whatever the situation, I can find the stillness. And if I allow myself to do that, slowly the number of thoughts diminishes. I become aware that there are spaces between them. If I neither cling to nor reject those thoughts and associated feelings, if I simply allow them to be, watching them come and go without preference, then I grow increasingly aware of the spaces – the nothingness, if you will, and increasingly aware that the thoughts arise out of that emptiness and return to the emptiness.

If that sounds boring then let me be clear. What we are talking about here is not the kind of emptiness where you might look into the biscuit tin and be disappointed to find that somebody has taken the last biscuit, nor the kind of emptiness you focus on when your car is almost without fuel and you need to refill it. The subject here is an emptiness that is the essence of everything. From this emptiness all thought arises. From this emptiness the transient, material world starts to crystallise and has its short-lived being.

If you can bring yourself to let go of the illusion, the thoughts, the emotion, the self-justifications, the entitlement, the desire, and let the emptiness take hold of you, that is when you discover that, as Adyashanti[8] says, the emptiness, is dancing. And it is singing and it is making music, for it is full of wonder and joy, so full that it is bursting into the song of the galaxies and the planets, the whales and the strata of the Earth, as it sparkles unceasingly and pours forth, unperturbed by your resistance and mine, undistracted by ego and identity, the illusion of separateness into which we have fled and revelled, until we stop fighting what we are and let go – let go of what we think we are good for and what we think is important, what we think is vital and what we think our immortality depends on. For when we unshackle ourselves from our failure-doomed determination to be what we are not, when we break out of the cage of self and become that nothingness, become the emptiness, then we start to realise that this is peace, this is joy, this is equanimity. This is what we have sought to regain ever since we made ourselves what we think we should be, what we think will be admired, what will reassure us that we actually are.

The emptiness is dancing for joy. It is dancing for love and it is dancing all that is into being. Discover this place and everything starts to change. You lose your preoccupation with material possessions, for why would you want that which is just illusion? You discover that the nature of this emptiness is pure love. This is the place from which compassion springs. This is where you start to realise you are not separate from all that is, you are of the same substance and the same being. You find that it is in the giving of that being that fulfilment arises. You start to discover that what you have been looking for all your life is not something but nothing. All you need to bring you peace and equanimity and that elusive thing we call happiness, is this nothing.

---

[8] Adyashanti: Emptiness Dancing

The boy admonished for staring out of the window never did quite get the hang of conjugating Latin verbs, nor did he ever derive much happiness from knowing that there was a square on the hypotenuse. But he did cultivate a habit of staring out of windows into the emptiness and thus came to learn that he was good-for-nothing. And that is what made all the difference.

So my question to you, therefore, is can you let yourself be good-for-nothing? If you have spent a lifetime trying, without success, to be good for something, trying to be good for a skill or expertise, trying to be good to please another person or many other persons, trying to be good enough to become satisfied with yourself, then instead, try this: letting go of all of that and, in the stillness of emptiness, become good-for-nothing. For you will discover that nothing is pure unadulterated love, that nothing is where the light is, that nothing is where the peace is. And then the dancing can begin.

30 The Sun Road

From a distant country the Sun is calling me by name. I have asked about these parts, but none can hear her as I do, nor can tell me how to find her land. So, being a traveller by nature, I have set forth upon an unmapped road, intent upon meeting the one who is calling me. Each footstep I set down is placed on unknown ground. Each corner that I turn leads to panoramas hitherto unseen.

At first, in confidence, I thought to call upon experience to guide me, for I have lived long and walked on many roads. But soon I realised that such maps as I carry are useless, being of ways I no longer pass.

Many other maps are offered me upon this road, drawn by those who would seek to profit from travellers such as me. These entice with stories of treasure, buried shallow by the roadside – untold wealth, enough to sate the lust of any. They promise to show me where to dig, if only I will give them all I own and pause upon my quest. I ask why, if they know where such riches are buried, they have not removed them long ago. None will answer me, and for all those I see digging, there seem few who ever find such treasure.

Others entreat me to turn back, crying, "On this road are dragons, consuming fires, terrors beyond the nightmares of madness." But pressing on, I have discovered that such dragons as I encounter are always much smaller than I imagined them to be. The fires exist, indeed, but are passable – with care. I have discovered that the greatest nightmares are not on the road, but in myself.

I have met some who claim that they, or some forefather of theirs have returned from the land to which I travel and purport to know the way, these make a living, of sorts, as guides. "Follow me they cry," or, more commonly, "Follow the one that I follow." But I am circumspect, noting that those who shout the loudest display most uncertainty in their eyes. At every danger they confront, their disciples turn back, weeping.

Then there are the brittle-hearted – cynical souls, who, having walked for many years and, still not finding this land, declare it merely myth, their time upon the road wasted. Having failed in their own quest, they are intent upon ending mine, fearing greatly that I, through perseverance, may find what they have not. To these, I simply bow and walk away.

Today, I happened on a pilgrim, his hooded head bent low, hands met before him in supplication. As we walked, I passed a pleasant hour with him in silence. I ventured brave and asked him if he knew the way and perhaps could lead me on my journey. He smiled with great kindness and said that he could tell me only of the way he had already passed. All that he would add was that to walk the Sun Road travellers should not seek instruction from guides before them on the way. Rather, they should seek the subtle light that can illuminate the map already placed behind their eyes.

So I closed my eyes and looked for the map of which he spoke. When I opened them, the pilgrim was gone and before me stood a choice of paths. Which I take remains a decision I must make alone.

When I might reach this land, I cannot say. All I know is that the Sun still speaks my name, ever whispering that I will find the way and that I have been there before, for it is the land of my birth.

I lie upon my face at night.
My sole intent: to seek the light.
And though I try with all my might
without a master who has sight
I cannot hope to find the light.
The darkness comes, I cry in fright.
The wind is howling in the night.
I sink into the storm of night.
I cry out, "Master, aid my sight.
Is there no ending to this night?"
I search the depth, I search the height
but though I try with all my might
I cannot see where lies the light.
Now filled with sorrow in the night
still no one comes to aid my plight.
At dawn there comes the rising light.
My master comes on waves of light
he looks at me with kindest sight,
says, "Let the darkness be the light."
And with illuminated sight
I see samsara is the night.
I see my master in the light.
I see my master is the light.

There is no Master, only light.
I see that I was always light.
There is no I. There is the light.

32 Change

When you have learned to accept everything
you can change anything.

33 Emptiness

I am not speaking of emptiness
not emptiness, I am of speaking
not of emptiness, speaking, I am
speaking of emptiness, I am not
emptiness speaking of not, I am
not am I: emptiness of speaking
speaking not of emptiness, I am
emptiness, not of speaking am I
of not speaking, I am emptiness
not I am, emptiness of speaking
not of speaking, emptiness I am

I
    am
       not
         speaking
            of

emptiness
I
am not of speaking

not am   emptiness speaking of I

not   speaking

      emptiness

34 Releasing Butterflies

It is early morning in late summer 2015. Most of the flowers have gone and the air is turning cooler. Autumn will soon have her way, muting the colours of the waning growth, preparing the trees for winter sleep. I am living in Martock, Somerset with my beloved hearing dog, Matt.

We are circumnavigating the village recreation ground, as is our morning habit. Progress is relatively slow. I am badly out of condition after two-and-a-half years of near intolerable stress. I weigh almost nineteen stone (over 260 pounds) and at five foot eight inches tall, I am morbidly obese. By contrast, at twelve years of age, Matt is still in excellent health and has a full zest for life. My constant fear though, is that I will lose him. Although we do not know it, he still has four years to go.

The stress has come from a two-and-a-half-year battle to save my business from deliberate destruction by politically motivated forces way beyond my power to resist. Never mind the industry accolades we had received. Forget the thousands of clients who had loved us, the hundreds of staff who had shared our vision. Ignore the banks that had bid for our business. We never had a chance of survival, for the behemoth had made his decision and the behemoth is inestimably powerful. He moves his tail like a tall cedar, while he drinks up rivers.[9] We fell before him. The bureaucrats won.

---

[9] Job 40: 17

Emotion washes over me as we make our way round the park; anger at events that were beyond my control; anger at those who knowingly initiated them; anger at myself for my weakness and ineptitude, my powerlessness in being unable to deal with them. I rage my affronted aphorisms into the silent morning air. "Why has this happened? Why now, after all this time, after I have put so much of my life into this vision?" Silence deluges from the sky. There are no answers.

The naysayers have circled, berating me with taunts of what I did not do but should have done; what I did do but should not have done; their vessels, blown by the winds of resentment over waves of anger, now wrecked upon the rocks of their own ransacked dreams.

I am enveloped by an arctic wind of my own powerlessness, my mean worthlessness. "Is there any good in me at all?" I call out, rhetorically.

"There is goodness in you," comes the unexpected answer from the still, small voice.

"Well, it must be buried deep," I retort in my anger, "because no one else can see it!"

The voice falls silent and I wheeze my way on round the park.

We are coming to the end of our walk now, approaching the car park and the pavilion, where the cricket players change into their kit. At the end of the path is a barrier that prevents the entry of unauthorised motor vehicles. You have to step to one side, close by the back wall of the pavilion, to be able to pass through the space for pedestrians.

As I do so, a slight movement at ground level catches my eye. As usual, Matt is running on ahead, but he turns to check I am following and, because I have stopped, he stops too. I look down to see a butterfly on the ground. It is late in the year and I am surprised it has lived this long. As I look more closely, it tries to flap its wings. It is then, I realise that it is caught in the remains of an old spider's web, attached to a dry leaf. Struggle as it may, the butterfly cannot extricate itself. Two thoughts pass through my mind simultaneously. The first, that this is nothing of importance. The butterfly will soon be dead anyway, with the coming of the cold. It is the way of nature and certainly none of my concern. The second, that I could put this poor creature out of its misery with one press of my foot.

I stand on the fulcrum of choice, like some Greek god, balanced between the two possibilities. And then the light dawns over Mount Olympus. I know what I will do. I reach down and pick up the leaf holding the spider's web. The butterfly sees my hand approach and flaps its wings in panic. In so doing, it frees itself and flies away. Thinking no more of the matter, momentarily, I walk on. But then the voice whispers again and says, "Not buried so deep as all that." I stand, statuesque in the illumination, tears of gratitude flooding my eyes.

Though I do not know it yet, progressively over the coming five years, I will receive a cochlear implant and learn how to hear again. I will shed eighty-four pounds. I will write seven books. They will circumnavigate the globe electronically, bringing tears and laughter, illuminating journeys, releasing other butterflies. And I will follow them at the more sedate pace of jet aircraft, to speak at conferences, universities, schools, television and radio studios. And all because a fearsome hand reached down to shake an old dry leaf and freed a butterfly from a spider's web.

35 Last

There will be a room because there is always a room. There will be long hanging drapes and there will be gentle music from an organ placed discreetly behind a screen. There will be candles and soft lights shining down and it will seem to some as though the air is shimmering. They will file in one by one with sombre faces. There will be silent tears, grey eyes and greyer hearts. Voices will murmur below the music, be it Bach or Handel or, if you prefer, Beethoven.

It will be a time for looking back because there is no looking forward, not yet, not yet. They will speak kind words and will find admirable deeds to remember. Will the words be true? Were the deeds ever as altruistic as they will be said to have been?

You will be there, of course, hovering above the open casket, listening to the fine words and enjoying the music as you watch the tears fall, satisfied that you were suitably loved and valued by those who have attended. But as you look down upon the congregation a thought will occur to you and you will ask yourself: *What did I do with the time? Was it worth it? Was there any gain, and to whose account can such gain as there was be ascribed?*

Naturally, there was instinct and the actions that emanated from instinct; an irrepressible urge to procreate, an equally profound urge to protect. But there were also choices, oh, so many choices. And consequences too, the planned and the anticipated, the random and the unpredicted, those events that in our ignorance we are apt to term Acts of God.

But always there will be that inescapable question: *What have I done of lasting value in a universe that is always changing?* Then will appear before you scales of balance hanging from a chain. You will reach out and clutch the chain confidently in your hand, holding the scales up high at arms length for all to see – as if all could see.

First, upon the right cup of the scales, you will load up your finest achievements, those acts of public note that you held to be admirable, those deeds undertaken in the knowledge that they were esteemed, while those you considered less than you looked on wide eyed, and those you needed to impress began to think of you as one of themselves. For the right cup of the scales will weigh heavy with those deeds, plummeting down under the weight of your goodness, the benefit you have brought the world. You will nod in satisfaction as you gaze upon them, dismissing the near empty, left cup of the scale as it rises high, so high it is barely visible. For who could worry about a few tiny mistakes when the weight of goodness held to your account is so massive? Your confidence buttressed, you will hold that balance high, with straightened arm and confident smile, as if everyone gathered before you could see it as clearly as you do. And as you watch with satisfaction you will say to yourself, *Is this not great Babylon that I have built by my mighty power?*10

And when you have looked enough and gorged enough and justified yourself enough, a voice will come, for a voice always does come – a voice strangely familiar, a voice you have heard before, a voice that, perhaps, you might have been hearing all your life. And that voice will ask just one simple question: *What of the other deeds?*

You will look confused for a moment and ask, *What other deeds?*

And the voice will reply, *Think not upon your acts of pharisaic generosity, painless gifts of ample wealth, alms distributed that others might applaud you for your altruism. For these are merely the accumulations of ego, buttresses of an uneasy, unearned confidence.*

And you will respond in exasperation, *That is not fair! Much of what I did was pure and well meant.*

Quite so, the voice will whisper, *quite so. But what of the deeds that were undertaken in darkness, when no one looked upon your acting hand. And what of the times you reached out in anger? What of the times you shrank back in fear? What of the times when you were asked for generosity that was not convenient or would not stand to your visible credit? The decisions made in silence; the deeds enacted in darkness. What of those? What of those choices of your solitude, when you acted only from character, when it was only your heart that was speaking.*

And as the voice continues to whisper, you will watch as, slowly, the right cup of the scales begins to rise. And as it rises, and as the left cup begins to fall a little, your arm will start to shake a little in uncertainty as your heart, your stilled, unbeating heart, grows uneasy. And you will want the voice to stop but the voice will not stop and will say, *Think further. Think, too, of those times when you climbed upon hands and hearts of others, stamping down upon the hope-filled and the aspiring, that you might give yourself a firmer foundation of unshakeable ascendency, the times when you justified your selfishness with excuses and covered your eyes so that you did not see what harm you did. What of those times?*

On and on the voice will speak. In growing uneasiness, you will watch as the right cup of the scale rises inexorably, the left cup descending to meet it at the balance point. And you will say to the voice, *Please stop now, for I see and acknowledge that I was not perfect.* But the voice does not stop. On and on it whispers, enumerating act after deed after thought, wish after desire after intention, as all the while the left side of the balance drops lower and the right side rises so high that you can no longer see it and your arm, your long-dead arm, is crying out in pain from the weight of deeds you bear. But you will not put it down, will you? For you must justify yourself by listing more good deeds. In panic now, you call out all that you can remember that is to your credit, so loud that the air about your coffin begins to crackle and those in the front row look up from their tears in surprise. But they see only empty air, only the dust as it hovers in the shafts of sunlight that stream in through the windows, high above.

Hush, they will comfort one another, *it is only static. Nothing to fear. Nothing to worry about.* But you know different. There is nothing static about what is happening here. There is unrelenting, unstoppable motion, as in your determination you pile the balance high with thoughts of more fine deeds you had planned to perform had you not been taken before your time. At last, as your agonised arm starts to droop from the weight of deeds and intentions it can no longer bear, the left side of the balance now drops a little lower. Relief comes upon you, your enthusiasm rising as you start to load still more promises upon the balance, declarations of altruistic acts you will undertake if only you are given another chance. On and on you load those promises upon the right-hand cup, thinking not of how you might ever perform so many good deeds should you ever be granted the chance again. Finally, under the weight of all those commitments, the right side falls to meet the left and the scale stands once more in balance under the weight of promised deeds that will take you many lifetimes to fulfil.

You are overcome with relief. Your exhausted arm, screaming out in pain, begins to lower the scales towards the floor. But as you do, the voice begins whispering of your shortcomings yet again. You watch in horror as the left cup once more drops lower. Fighting back your pain in panic once again, you lift the balance still higher. The air about you crackles unmistakably, as the light begins to shimmer and you almost appear to the more sensitive members of the congregation. You roar out still more promises of good deeds to come, forgiveness to be offered, gifts of alms that will be given to the poor, oblivious to the impossibility of discharging your obligations, even if you were to live a further thousand lifetimes.

But, sure enough, the cups of the scales return to balance yet again – but only until you attempt to lower them to the floor again, whereupon the voice recommences its whispers. And now, in a moment of terrified insight you understand that this is hell and that you have lived in hell all through this last lifetime and for who knows how many other lifetimes before it. You begin to weep, your sorrow growing until your tears become a river, such that none could console you.

Finally, as you weep in misery beyond measure, the whispering voice takes on form and stands before you, a short robed figure, neither male nor female but somehow both and the figure fixes their eyes upon you, waiting for you to compose yourself. Eventually, you cease your weeping and realise that as long as you hold the gaze of the Whisperer, the pain in your arm becomes manageable. Without releasing this gaze, you lower the balance gently to the floor, in desperate hope that the Whisperer will remain silent. You are aware that the congregation is filing out at the end of the service now. No one has seen the scales, nor the battle you have been fighting to preserve your self-worth. With the congregation gone, the room begins to fade, leaving you and the Whisperer standing on a vast savannah, where a gentle dawn wind is moving across the grass. You are aware of the promises you have made that stand, mountain high, and you know it will take many lifetimes for you to discharge the obligations you have placed upon yourself. And you are aware, too, of the mountain of negativity that stands next to it and to this mountain you ascribe the name *karma*.

Strangely, though, the Whisperer seems somehow less focused on the balance and the cups and the mountains than you are as they look past you, now. Hoping desperately that they will not start speaking again of your many misdeeds, you take the chance of turning and following their gaze. Before you, you see a wall rising up, higher than the mountain of your promises, higher than the mountain of your karma, higher than your eye can see. As you try to take it in, the Whisperer walks past you and in so doing says,

Out beyond ideas of wrongdoing and rightdoing,
there is a field. I'll meet you there.[10]

In a moment the Whisperer passes through the wall and is gone, leaving you alone. Forgetting the balance and the cups and the

[10] Rumi: A Great Wagon

mountain of promises behind you, you kneel and kiss the ground. But though part of you wants to lie down in the grass, you know that the world is too full to talk about and that you must not go back to sleep, for the breeze has secrets to tell you*10*. You begin to search for a way to follow the Whisperer, for you know now it is your destiny to meet them again in that field, the field that lies beyond ideas of wrongdoing and right doing, though you cannot yet say what such a place might look like. Then, as if speaking through the wall, the voice comes again and says,

The door is round and open.
Don't go back to sleep.[11]

You begin searching for that door. You know that, however many lifetimes it takes, you will look for it until you find it. For above all, you are certain beyond any possible doubt that you will find it and that when you do you will pass through it. For entering that field will be like coming to the orchard in Spring.[12]

---

[11] Rumi: A Great Wagon
[12] Daniel 4:30

36 Lamplighters

The sun is high now and we see the road more clearly than we ever have before.

In the half-light of early dawn we had stumbled, stumbled many times upon the boulders and the rocky twists of the path that led upward, ever upward. We had wanted to stop, of course. We had wanted to turn back. It was too hard, too demanding. Clearly, this path had been set for others. But us? Surely not. We were meant for easier roads, paved, level, flat. Who in their right mind would take such a path as this, when smoother, gentler options stood open and inviting?

There had been many fellow travellers at the start. Our band was joyful at the prospect of new countries, new experiences, new pleasures. But with each unpredictable turn in the path, each jagged boulder to be negotiated, companions fell away. Some simply turned back, the demands of the climb being beyond them. Some fell from the road, tumbling into the ravines and caverns that stretched out below us. And of all of these, we never saw nor heard again. Finally, there were just we two. Bonded in the fellowship of travel we journey on, ruggedised, oblivious now to the difficulty of the road, the soreness of our feet, the weariness of our limbs.

For inside ourselves, we knew. We did not want to know. We would have much preferred never to have known. But each time we made as if to turn back, the voice of the Guide called us onward, upward, encouraging us to map the path, that others might follow where we had travelled and their journey might thus be made clearer, faster than our own.

As the sun rose to its zenith, the heat of the day set in. It is easier to see now, and our past mistakes, our mis-turns, our trips and falls have become lamentable to us. We had been such novices when we started. We wonder how we had ever progressed at all.

But in the illumination of the midday sun, with understanding comes also the heat of challenge. The climb becomes harder, not because the path is steeper (though who could say it is not?) but because we understand now that the journey demands focus, determination, commitment.

We are climbers by nature, you and I. We have always climbed. Climbing is all we know. We climb, because we cannot not climb. We map because it is our vocation to map; though we have not always known it so, we cartographers of the heart, we road-mappers of soul.

And now that the heat of the day has passed, we see the nature and purpose of the journey. With the lengthening of the shadows, we have come to realise that time is growing short. We see the destination that must be reached the day is done and darkness falls. We climb on to the summit, placing our roadmaps carefully at selected points on the path, that others might know the route and take heart that this way has been trodden before.

Will you journey on with me? The summit is calling. Do not abandon me now, when we are so close. As evening falls, light my lamp for me as I will light yours for you. For see, we have become lamplighters.

37 Last Dogs

"Have you done Last Dogs?" you ask, just after I have turned out the light and am settling down in the dark, trying to find space amongst the ten legs on the bed that do not belong to me. Eight of them refuse to budge to accommodate my arrival. It is remarkable to me how intrusively attentive dogs can be when they want something, how infuriatingly apathetic when they do not want to be disturbed. I groan because, no, I have not done Last Dogs.

I get out of bed, throw on my dressing gown and call out, "Come on you two," as I flick the light switch over the little winding staircase. Chase End, our two-hundred-year-old cottage in the north of the New Forest, used to be the village bakery. I make my way carefully down under the low beam, noting once again that nineteenth century bakers were either remarkably short or particularly hard-headed. I pass the enormous inglenook in the lounge, which still boasts the tiny pay window through which customers would pass their payment before collecting their bread at the door. As I reach the door, I am overtaken by Matt and Betty, our hearing dogs. They have abandoned their comatose state on the bed, preferring anticipated encounters with the night-emboldened forest creatures that visit our garden.

The open door frees them into the faintest of light from a waning crescent moon. I have hopes that they will return quickly of their own accord. No such luck. Matt finds his way back within seconds but after a minute or more, I am still calling Betty, resigned already to the certainty that she will continue to ignore me. I pick up a torch and her lead and step out, slipper-shod, into the winter night, where she is criss-crossing the garden. She runs provocatively through the torch beam. Can dogs be provocative? This one definitely can, determined to evade capture, determined to assert her alpha status. It is a nightly ritual. Eventually, and only when she has had enough, she runs into the house, ignoring me. By the time I get back to bed all three of you are asleep and ten legs are once again entwined in a conspiratorial lattice, designed to repel my bid for a paltry share of the space. How can one slightly built human female and two small dogs manage to take up the whole of a super-king bed? It remains one of the unanswered ontological questions of the cosmos.

"Have you done Last Dogs?" you ask, as I settle down in the dark. Space is easier to come by on the super-king, now that there are only six legs that do not belong to me. We both yearn for it to be otherwise. After more than six years of unbroken companionship, Hearing Dogs For Deaf People have taken back Betty, your black cockerpoo due to 'unexpected ill health.' No recipient ever actually owns a hearing dog. The charity always retains legal ownership and removes dogs when they see a need to do so. But that one small statement overlays an emotional entanglement that we could spend the rest of a lifetime documenting. Only we won't. We will cry into the silence and purport to move on, now that we are left only with Matt, my beloved spaniel-cross. At fourteen years of age, he is now retired and therefore effectively beyond the threat of removal.

Matt is too old to be permitted to jump down onto his arthritis-ravaged legs, so I lift him gently from the bed and attach his lead to his collar. I walk him out into the darkness behind the block of flats where we now live. Some years back, we moved out of the New Forest and into New Milton, just too far the wrong side of the cattle grid for my liking, due to what I euphemistically called, 'a change of circumstances.' Financial devastation has hit, requiring that I rein in expenditure, batten down hatches, tighten belts, make do and mend. All of the usual clichés and more apply. At first, I railed in fury at the unjustified devastation of my comfort zone. But eventually I worked my way through that anger and acknowledged that my life came with no guarantees, nor any promise of fairness. I have taken less interest in material possessions for years now, anyway, walking a path that is increasingly focused on the light of and the journey to the light. Only the absence of the Forest itself from my daily routines perturbs me. But I still live close enough to walk there daily when I am willing to take the trouble to do so.

Matt still walks with me as best he is able and will do so until the end of his days. To be parted now would be unthinkable. But he is old and the arthritis has finally reached all four of his limbs. He moves as little as possible and would just as soon stay on the bed and pee onto the quilt if I allowed him. But that's non-negotiable – other than when I forget to do Last Dogs. The consequences of such memory lapses are always unpleasant and time consuming. So, we are out here on the back lawn where, under the illumination of the porch light, he squats. Cocking his leg causes too much pain now, another consequence of arthritis. Does a male dog in such circumstances find it demeaning to be forced to pee in the same way as a female, I wonder? Matt was never an alpha dog, though. Never what you might call macho, he has always been the card drawn from the bottom of the pack, the least assertive dog of the litter.

His world has contracted steadily, year by year. Gone are the days of his youth, spent charging through the undergrowth in some Forest Inclosure, well beyond my sight, terrifying me with the prospect that he will encounter something larger and more aggressive than himself. Gone, even, are the days of running, free of the lead, around the local recreation ground. Loss of both sight and hearing mean he would not find his way back to me and could easily bolt instinctively for home, which lies across two busy roads. So he walks slowly and close to me whenever I can persuade him out into the open air. Our walks now extend to no more than a couple of hundred yards, as he sways uncertainly around the garden of our block of flats. But even this short distance can take us as long as two or three miles used to. For he walks so slowly now, stopping every few yards to take long, slow inhalations from the ground, as if invoking the spectral resurrection of rabbit chases past. I do not think he can smell any better than he can see or hear. But we carry on as best we can, sustaining the rituals that support his continued desire to live. I am determined to make these last few weeks a love offering towards him, repaying some of the inestimable debt that I have accumulated for all of the hearing support, the joy, the happiness and laughter that he has brought to me over the last fifteen years.

Have I done Last Dogs? My question is self-posed, silent. I am terrified that I might have. When does a momentary lapse of concentration become negligence? At what point does rote become stupidity? I am berating myself for my foolishness with these and other questions as I drive at well over the speed limit to an emergency vet appointment. We have been staying in West Bay, at an apartment on the sea front that belongs to our friends, Richard and Sue. This morning, I had attached Matt's lead and walked him the short distance to the pedestrianised area at the western end of the esplanade. It stands some three metres above the level of the beach. My mind has wandered to something utterly unimportant and, oblivious to the consequences, I have released the lead from his collar. I have done so because, here, I have always released his lead from his collar to let him walk in safety. The area is traffic-free, for sure. But some environments that have been safe all his life now pose danger. I am unforgivably negligent of the fact that he can no longer see the drop to the beach. The railing at the precipice is set at a height to ensure human safety. But there is nothing to stop a small dog from walking underneath it. Unaware of the consequences, he steps too close. Just at the moment I awaken to the danger and move forward to avert it, he falls three metres. My heart falls three thousand miles. I look down over the railings. He has fallen onto his side and is lying motionless on the sand. My jaw drops and my eyes widen. My panic is screaming at me. I run to the steps some thirty metres away, charge down them, then tear back at the same pace to the point where he is lying. But by the time I arrive he is standing, still alive and with nothing obviously broken, merely looking dazed and obviously wondering how he got here. When he seems ready, I walk him back to the foot of the steps, checking the whole time whether he is limping or in any discomfort. He seems okay. I carry him up the steps – not too much of a challenge with a twelve-kilo dog – then set him down on the promenade. I check a hundred times that he is absolutely, definitely, unmistakably attached to his lead. Then I continue to watch him carefully as I text the vet's surgery to explain the situation. They recommend bringing him in immediately. But we are an hour-and-a-half away.

So now I am checking the rear-view mirror, not for police cars or anything outside my vehicle, but for the wellbeing of my beloved dog. He is sitting on the back seat with a distant look in his eyes when he vomits. I screech the car to a halt, certain that he is about to die. But he does not die. I clean him up and stroke him gently. He does not react with any obvious discomfort. We continue the journey for the rest of the interminable forty miles until finally we arrive at the vet's – an all too familiar location to us, for, at his advanced age, we are visiting frequently. The long-suffering vet checks him over but there is no apparent damage. She soothes my agony, telling me only to watch him carefully.

Later that evening, I text my friend Sue, who has decades of experience of living and working with dogs. "Have I killed my dog?" I ask. The response is almost immediate and terrifyingly non-committal. "You will know in forty-eight hours." I sleep little that night, waking repeatedly to reach out and touch him, checking that he is still breathing, wishing desperately for the god of time to accelerate us past that forty-eight-hour deadline, when his survival might just grant me absolution for my stupidity. In the morning he is still with me. A further day and night tick by without apparent ill consequence. I am astonished that this frail creature of sixteen years of age is sufficiently resilient to pass through such an experience apparently unscathed. But Matt is not ready to leave us yet.

Have I done Last Dogs? Today, although we do not know it, he will pay his penultimate visit to the vet. We have been through acupressure and laser treatments by the dozen, examinations and tests by the score, administered a whole pharmacy-worth of medication. I tell the vet that I neither want his life ended prematurely for my convenience, nor preserved to his unnecessary discomfort for the postponement of my own pain. All that counts is my beloved dog's welfare. She looks at me with great sympathy and says, simply, "Then we are on the same page." We both know that the page we are on is almost the last in the book. It is a page that I would give anything, yes, literally anything, not to have to turn.

We return to the surgery some days later for his twice-weekly acupressure. But this time, the moment that the nurse sees him, a pained expression crosses her face. She mumbles something about needing to get the vet, who then enters the treatment room to examine him and tell me what I already knew she would say: today is his last day. Today we must do Last Dogs. I return to the car to fetch you, as I know you will want to be there too.

Long ago I was told that what dogs most want when their time of passing arrives is the presence of their guardians. I have long since decided that I will be present for him in as literal and comprehensive a way as I possibly can. We enter the treatment room and I lift him onto the table for the last time. He is calm. He is peaceful. He is aching with pain. The vet explains that she will first insert a cannula into his front leg and then administer a pre-med to relax him. Finally, she will give him the last injection. With the utmost gentleness, she cleans and shaves his leg. Then, with love as evident as her expertise, she inserts the cannula. He does not flinch. My hands are about his head and body now, caressing him, stroking him. I am whispering to him as the cosmos revolves timelessly, inexplicably, about his sadness and my agony. I squat before him at the front of the table, looking as deeply as I can into his eyes. He looks back at me with a mixture of love and gratitude, gratitude that he does not owe me. It is I who am in debt. I owe this creature inestimably more than I will ever be able to repay. To desert him at his time of departure would be unthinkable. As the vet administers the life-ending injection, I hold his head with my hands and his gaze with my eyes, all the while telling him that I love him. My tears run as free as his spirit is about to run. His eyes close for the last time. I continue to stroke his head, still squatting in front of him. I am all but kneeling in worship.

From somewhere far away comes a voice telling me that his heart has stopped beating. The vet leaves the room. I hold him and whisper love to him as his consciousness slips away. Some time later – I have no idea how long – she returns to hold a one-sided conversation with me, during which she explains that his body will be cremated and, as I have requested, the ashes returned to me in about two weeks.

"Shall we do last dogs?" I ask you. This day has been marked on the calendar, planned for sometime. We had lived with those ashes for several weeks, neither of us inclined to let them leave our charge, neither of us willing yet to let him go. But today is the appointed day. We put on boots and jackets, you pick up your walking stick and I pick up the box that holds all that remains of Matt – all, that is, except the presence of the creature we love most. That lingers on, inside us and around us, drifting like perfume through our home, attending every walk, still sleeping each night upon a bed that is far too empty. I hate that I do not have to fight for space. Four legs will never be enough.

Once again, I point the car north towards the old familiar destination of Godshill Wood. The journey seems somehow surreal, otherly, as if happening to someone else. We slip in and out of conversation, talking of nothing of great consequence. It is a non-conversation, an avoidance strategy to soften our awareness of an ending that must come but is oh, so unwelcome.

We park in the gravel car park and enter the Inclosure via the little swing gate. Before us lies the old familiar pathway that winds into the wood. By now, Matt would have been bounding on ahead of us, rushing this way and that, overwhelmed with the excitement of space and freedom and opportunity. Godshill Wood has been my favourite part of the New Forest since we were fortunate enough, years ago, to live within walking distance of its swaying canopies. In those days, we would mount the hill from our little thatched cottage on the valley floor, Matt racing ahead. When did he stop doing that? When was it that exuberance gave way to the slow, sedate pace of eldership, to the inexorable creep of arthritis, to the relentless decline that is old age? I loved him more the older he grew.

The path is narrow and we cannot walk side by side. You let me lead, in order to give me the chance to choose our destination – though at this moment I do not know precisely where we are bound. I carry the box in both hands in front of me, you walking behind. We are a little funeral procession. Heading north, we cross over the wide gravel path that runs east-west through the Inclosure, preferring to feel the Forest floor beneath our feet, choosing the paths less travelled by– unless you count the rabbits and the foxes and the Dryads that shepherd the trees. I have grown used to feeling and, occasionally, seeing these creatures and was surprised to have no awareness of them as we entered the wood from the car park. About us, the silence grows tangible. You could cut it with a knife. But why would you want to? No knife is necessary for a ritual such as this.

Thus we proceed, penetrating deeper into the wood, until we round a bend and I know, instantly, that this is the place. And yes, here I do sense the dryads, congregated about a large mature oak tree that stands on a grass island in the middle of the path. It is in this place that his remains will mingle with the Forest. There could be no other.

Both you and the dryads stand back a little way, while I step onto the grass beneath the branches of the tree. I open the box and take out the little plastic bag with the last remains of the dearest friend I have ever known and, in all likelihood, ever will know. I am about to upend and shake the bag but stop, realising that such a swift act is too abrupt to mark the finality of the occasion. I need to engage more intimately with him on this, our last physical encounter. I shake the bag gently, allowing his ashes to pour slowly through my open fingers, watching in silence as the grey dust wafts to the ground, mingling with my tears. I stand here, transfixed, as the last of his energy infuses with that of the Forest. Then I stand aside to allow you to move forward into this secret, sacred space. You inscribe Reiki symbols into the air above his resting place, your lips moving in a silent incantation that invokes protection, your tears adding to those I have already shed. When you are done, we smile softly at each other, then turn and walk away. The silence remains unbroken. Who could want it otherwise?

"Shall we do Last Dogs?" It is exactly one year since the sprinkling and we have decided to revisit his resting place. Neither of us has really let go of him over these last twelve months. You are more sensitive than I am, often seeing what I do not. From time to time, you tell me when he is here in the flat with us, or when he walks behind us on a stroll. But I do not see him. For such information I rely on you, a spirit who sees into the unseen more easily than I.

So we drive the same route back up to Godshill Wood as we did precisely a year before. We stand at the site of his sprinkling for as long as our hearts desire and our tears need, then return to the lawn outside the Inclosure, where we spread a blanket on the ground and enjoy a picnic in the sunshine. Afterwards, as we walk, you tell me he is following just a little way behind.

Have we done Last Dogs? It is two years on and he visits less now, you say. We decide that we will return to Godshill Wood once again. But when we arrive at the car park, there is a notice informing of us that tree felling is taking place in the Inclosure. A padlock and strong chain block our entry, preventing our visiting him. Instead, we walk on the lawn outside. As we wander through the July sunshine, you tell me he is walking behind us, though at a greater distance than has been his former habit. And then you look back one final time. You tell me that he has turned and is walking away. I do not respond. I know now that I will not return again to his resting place until my own ashes are scattered there. For, until that time, he has done Last Dogs.

Gallery/Biographical

Photograph by Minnie Harding

Michael Forester writes at the fulcrum of perceived reality. His works range from the inspirational and provocative *Forest Rain* to the book-length metaphorical epic poem *Dragonsong*; from his exploration of our endangered planet in the travelogue *One Journey,* to the ever-popular story of his first year with his hearing dog, Matt, *If It Wasn't For That Dog.*

His books are followed worldwide, from Australia to California, from the Philippines to Wales. A profoundly deaf full time author and public speaker, Michael is 67 years old. He lives in the UK between the southern edge of the New Forest and the sea from where he travels internationally to speak publically and sign his books for readers.

Michael's own life journey has taken him from formative years in charismatic Christianity, through a miraculously survived suicide attempt and into a spiritual awakening, through the onset of profound deafness and the life-changing arrival of a hearing dog. He has travelled the planet from the Amazon rainforest to South Africa, from the Himalayas to the Philippines and beyond.

Michael Forester's books are available at his website **www.michaelforester.co.uk** and on Amazon. To order signed copies of Michael's books or request speaking engagements email **michaelforesterauthor@gmail.com**

Other Books by Michael Forester

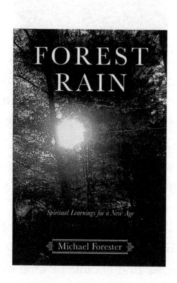

This unique collection of essays, metaphors and verse has been called one of the great books of all time, a book that will open doors in your heart and mind. Here, you will find:

The soul awakening that follows a near death experience

The unseen protectors who are always about us, guiding our life journey

The love we pursue relentlessly until we realise that it was always seeking us

Forest Rain will lead you on a journey into your own soul, to face your fears, your regrets and your life purpose and so to find the love that has always awaited you.

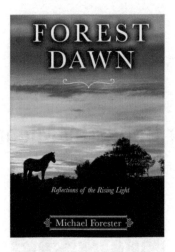

In this, his second collection of inspirational essays, metaphors and poetry, Michael Forester illuminates the profound that hides in the simple and the eternal that shines through the commonplace.

A man tries to buy peace by the pound... a child learns the transience of life when he treads on a spider... angels appear just when needed.

Here, we encounter the healing power of our dreams and the lessons that dancing holds for life's journey... a life-changing confrontation with a beggar... what we find because of what we lose.

Forest Dawn will make you laugh and it will make you cry. But most of all, it will bring you face-to-face with the person who can teach you most: yourself.

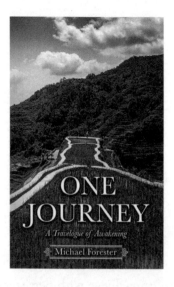

There is only One Journey. We commence it the moment we enter the physical world and complete it the moment we leave. Our journey is travelled on a road of self-discovery. During that journey, we may take many trips, make many voyages. Here are four, undertaken over a period of fourteen years:

* In the Amazon rainforest, a confrontation with the unceasing exploitation of its resources and people.

* In South Africa, an encounter with the power of forgiveness, fifteen years after the ending of apartheid.

* In Nepal and the Himalayas, a pilgrimage of self-discovery.

* In the Philippines, an exploration of the impact of economic modernisation upon the people and the land.

Each explores how, if we have the eyes to see and the ears to hear, our voyages into the world are, in reality, a reflection of our journey into ourselves.

IF IT WASN'T FOR THAT DOG!

MICHAEL FORESTER

It's amazing what you can achieve with persistence, a bit of chopped liver and a second hand teddy bear....

In 2002 Michael, a deafened man from the New Forest, lost his home, his marriage, his business and his father – but he can't actually remember if it was in that order. However, in the same year someone suggested that getting a dog might be a good idea – not just any dog, but a hearing dog from Hearing Dogs for Deaf People. And when, in 2004, Michael was presented with a hearing dog of his own called Matt, he just *knew* life would be so much easier. Amazing how wrong you can be, isn't it!

If It Wasn't For That Dog is the story of Matt's first year with Michael, the challenges and accomplishments of climbing the hearing-dog learning curve, the profound changes he stimulated and the inestimable joy he confers magically on everyone who meets him. But most of all it is the story of the strange power of meaty treats to work miracles in doggie behaviour.

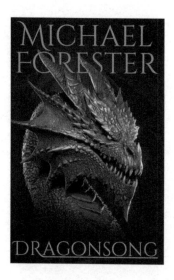

Rebekah, daughter of Merlin and noblewoman of Albion, has been driven to madness by the murder of her lover, Vidar. In her torment she bargains with the Prince of Demons to turn her into a dragon. Once so transformed, she seeks to take revenge upon her father, Merlin, for she has been fooled into believing he is responsible for Vidar's death. Behind the subterfuge stands Oberon, Captain-King of Elves, who cannot foresee the devastation his jealousy and unrequited love for Rebekah will unleash upon the world of Gaia. Its salvation depends upon the retrieval of the Sleep Stone from the gates of Hell. But if the stone is not returned, the demon army will awaken and ransack Gaia in a war that will destroy it. Time is the solution – but only if the gods of Asgard can find a way of stopping it.

the

goblin child

*and other
stories*

MICHAEL FORESTER

Well hello there.

Why don't you step inside and take a look round? You remember this place, don't you? That's right. You've been here before. And us. Surely you remember us. We're old friends. This is where the light in your eyes glimpses the darkness in your mind. Sit down and stay a while – if you can face the risk of finding out who you really are, that is. I'll introduce you to some friends of mine:

Come meet the man who remembers his birth. He wishes he didn't. And the goblin child – if his mother is to be believed, that is. Or how about the boy who takes his god to school? And Santa. You really wouldn't want to leave without meeting Santa, would you? But really it's all about David, you understand, who spent his life circling the moon – just like you and I do, in fact. Come with me. Come with me now.

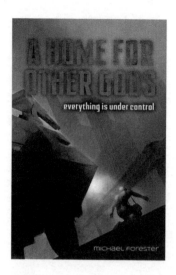

It's 2117 in a country where everything you do has to be approved by the state; a state that tells you what to eat, when to shower, when to make love, what to think. As the waters rise in the city, the fish people begin to arrive. Utterly compliant, they open and close their mouths incessantly, saying nothing. When Greg dares to think for himself, the Departmental Republic seeks to draw him into their elite to keep him quiet. But if he agrees, it's going to cost him his home and the life of his family.

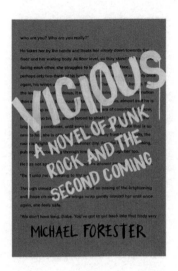

VICIOUS

A NOVEL OF PUNK
ROCK AND THE
SECOND COMING

MICHAEL FORESTER

For thirty years, Tolly's been waiting for the reincarnation of rock star Sid Vicious who's definitely coming back to love her forever. Now that she's certain she's found him in the form of young Henry, well, Henry's girlfriend Laura has to be stalked and eliminated, doesn't she?

But... something's not right. Because when Tolly kidnaps Laura, hovering in the background are unearthly wispy creatures – *Ethereals*, they call themselves. Is this some kind of a game? Could Laura really be miraculously pregnant with the second coming of the Messiah, as her Pastor, Philemon Littlemann insists? Or is she just as insane as Tolly?

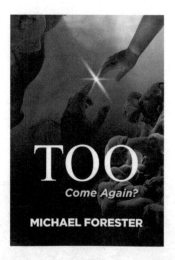

TOO
Come Again?

MICHAEL FORESTER

* What do you do when your daughter is murdered during childbirth?

* What do you do when you're told your grandchild is the second coming of The Messiah?

* What do you do when powerful forces seek to take that child to exploit it?

* What do you do when you alone know the secret the child carries that proves its divinity?

What do you do?

You run.

Photograph by Minnie Harding